TEXT & PERFORMANCE

Hamlet

Peter Davison

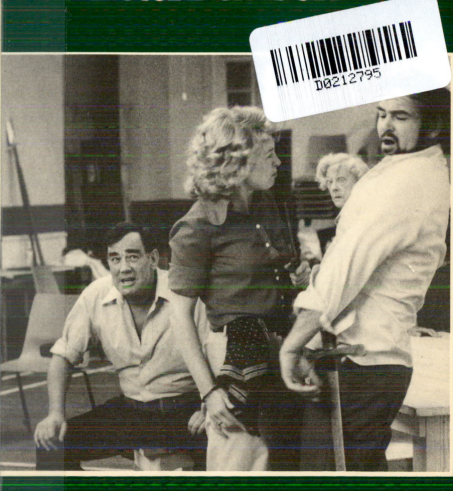

TEXT AND PERFORMANCE

General Editor: Michael Scott

The series is designed to introduce sixth-form and undergraduate students to the themes, continuing vitality and performance of major dramatic works. The attention given to production aspects is an element of special importance, responding to the invigoration given to literary study by the work of leading contemporary critics.

The prime aim is to present each play as a vital experience in the mind of the reader – achieved by analysis of the text in relation to its themes and theatricality. Emphasis is accordingly placed on the relevance of the work to the modern reader and the world of today. At the same time, traditional views are presented and appraised, forming the basis from which a creative response to the text can develop.

In each volume, Part One: *Text* discusses certain key themes or problems, the reader being encouraged to gain a stronger perception both of the inherent character of the work and also of variations in interpreting it. Part Two: *Performance* examines the ways in which these themes or problems have been handled in modern productions, and the approaches and techniques employed to enhance the play's accessibility to modern audiences.

A Synopsis of the play is given and an outline of its major sources and a concluding Reading List offers guidance to the student's independent study of the work.

PUBLISHED

A Midsummer Night's Dream	Roger Warren
Antony and Cleopatra	Michael Scott
Hamlet	Peter Davison
Henry the Fourth, Parts I and II	T. F. Wharton

IN PREPARATION

Doctor Faustus	William Tydeman
King Lear	Gamini Salgādo
Macbeth	Gordon Williams
Measure for Measure	Graham Nicholls
Othello	Martin L. Wine
The Tempest	David Hirst
The Winter's Tale	R. P. Draper
Twelfth Night	Lois Potter
Volpone	Arnold Hinchliffe

HAMLET

Text and Performance

PETER DAVISON

First published 1983 by
THE MACMILLAN PRESS LTD
Companies and representatives
throughout the world

ISBN 0 333 33994 0 (pbk)

Typeset by
WESSEX TYPESETTERS LTD,
Frome, Somerset

Printed in Hong Kong

CONTENTS

Illustrations appear in Part Two

6

ACKNOWLEDGEMENTS

The author is indebted to the sources given in the Reading List for valuable information; to the Folger Shakespeare Library, Washington, D.C., for enabling him to see the filmed version of the Gielgud/Burton *Hamlet*; and to The British Academy for enabling him to study at the Folger.

Quotations of the text of the play are from the New Penguin Shakespeare edition (1980), edited by T. J. B. Spencer.

Source-details for the illustrations are given with the relevant captions.

FOR
AMELIA

GENERAL EDITOR'S PREFACE

For many years a mutual suspicion existed between the theatre director and the literary critic of drama. Although in the first half of the century there were important exceptions, such was the rule. A radical change of attitude, however, has taken place over the last thirty years. Critics and directors now increasingly recognise the significance of each other's work and acknowledge their growing awareness of interdependence. Both interpret the same text, but do so according to their different situations and functions. Without the director, the designer and the actor, a play's existence is only partial. They revitalise the text with action, enabling the drama to live fully at each performance. The academic critic investigates the script to elucidate its textual problems, understand its conventions and discover how it operates. He may also propose his view of the work, expounding what he considers to be its significance.

Dramatic texts belong therefore to theatre and to literature. The aim of the 'Text and Performance' series is to achieve a fuller recognition of how both enhance our enjoyment of the play. Each volume follows the same basic pattern. Part One provides a critical introduction to the play under discussion, using the techniques and criteria of the literary critic in examining the manner in which the work operates through language, imagery and action. Part Two takes the enquiry further into the play's theatricality by focusing on selected productions of recent times so as to illustrate points of contrast and comparison in the interpretation of different directors and actors, and to demonstrate how the drama has worked on the modern stage. In this way the series seeks to provide a lively and informative introduction to major plays in their text and performance.

MICHAEL SCOTT

PLOT SYNOPSIS AND SOURCES

Hamlet's father has died and his uncle, Claudius, has ascended the Danish throne, incestuously marrying the Queen, Gertrude. Watch is being kept for a Norwegian attack but it is the Ghost of Hamlet's father who appears. The Ghost charges Hamlet with exacting revenge for his murder by Claudius. Hamlet believes the Ghost is 'honest' but has reservations. We see Claudius's court and hear of Fortinbras of Norway's intentions. Polonius, a seemingly amusing old counsellor, advises his son, Laertes, about behaviour in Paris, whilst Laertes advises his sister, Ophelia, about Hamlet.

Polonius briefs a servant to spy on Laertes, and Claudius briefs two old friends of Hamlet, Rosencrantz and Guildenstern, to spy on Hamlet. Polonius acquires a letter Hamlet has written to Ophelia and reveals its contents to Claudius and Gertrude. Hamlet is suspicious of Rosencrantz and Guidenstern but delighted at the arrival of a troupe of actors. He proposes to have a play performed to test the Ghost's claim that Claudius murdered his father.

Hamlet's growing despair and disgust become increasingly apparent. Ophelia has been 'loosed' to betray Hamlet who, realising this, turns on her viciously. The actors perform and the King's perturbation convinces Hamlet of his guilt. He refrains from killing Claudius at prayer for that would merely despatch him heavenwards. He tries to persuade his mother to admit her faults; hearing a noise and believing Claudius is spying on him, he kills Polonius by mistake. The Ghost reappears, demanding action, being seen only by Hamlet.

Claudius arranges for Hamlet to be sent to England and there executed, but he escapes. Ophelia becomes insane and drowns. Laertes returns vowing vengeance, and Claudius arranges a duel, supposedly in sport, during which Hamlet will be murdered. The plan miscarries; the Queen drinks poison and Laertes is wounded with a poison-baited rapier, both intended for Hamlet. Hamlet kills Claudius and is himself fatally wounded. Fortinbras, returned from an attack on Poland, enters and assumes command.

SOURCES

Threads of the story – some going back to pre-literary times – were drawn together in Saxo Grammaticus's *Historia Danica* (Paris, 1514). Belleforest's French version, *Histoires Tragiques* (1570) may have been known to Shakespeare; but his immediate source was an earlier play about Hamlet (now lost) – termed by scholars the *Ur-Hamlet* – probably by Thomas Kyd, which had a revival in 1594. For 'The Murder of Gonzago' (the play-within-the-play) and the mode of Hamlet's father's death, he may have drawn on the Duke of Urbino's murder in 1538, instigated by Luigi Gonzaga.

PART ONE: TEXT

1 INTRODUCTION

Mortality and Amusement

> . . . in the tragedy of *Hamlet* . . . the ghost of a king appears on the
> stage . . . Hamlet becomes crazy in the second act, and his mistress
> becomes crazy in the third; the prince slays the father of his mistress
> under the pretence of killing a rat, and the heroine throws herself
> into the river; a grave is dug on the stage, and the gravediggers talk
> quodlibets worthy of themselves, while holding skulls in their
> hands; Hamlet responds to their nasty vulgarities in silliness no less
> disgusting. In the meanwhile another of the actors conquers
> Poland. Hamlet, his mother, and his father-in-law, carouse on the
> stage; songs are sung at table; there is quarrelling, fighting, killing –
> one would imagine this piece to be the work of a drunken savage.

Yes, this is the same play as that described in the Synopsis.
What is more, this is an account of Shakespeare's *Hamlet* by one
of the greatest writers of the eighteenth century: Voltaire,
philosopher, dramatist, musician, scientist – and satirist. *Hamlet*, he wrote in 1748, 'is a vulgar and barbarous drama, which
would not be tolerated by the vilest populace of France, or
Italy'. Nor was Voltaire alone, at least among Frenchmen. In
the whole of the eighteenth century there was only one production of *Hamlet* in France (in 1769) and that a pale reflection,
lacking Ophelia's mad scene, a ghost (his instructions were
reported), the visiting actors, and the gravediggers. These were
all instances of what the adapter, Jean-François Ducis,
described to David Garrick (whose version will be discussed
later) as 'savage irregularities'.

It is easy to laugh at such a view of a play that has had
incomparable success throughout the world for nearly 400
years. It can be put down to a curious paradox in Anglo-French
attitudes in the eighteenth century to which a French writer,

Simon Linguet, drew attention in 1777 after seeing *Hamlet* in London. The audience of men and women, girls and sailors, lawyers, merchants and lords (note the heterogeneity, something we too readily associate only with Shakespeare's Globe), were in ecstasy, he wrote, laughing and applauding, despite a final scene of body piled on body. How marked was the contrast between what was witnessed on stage with 'la douceur des loix penales' – the gentleness of the English penal laws (even though this was the eighteenth century!). In France, said Linguet, it was the reverse: all refinement on stage, harsh cruelty in life. As with all travellers' observations, this is an oversimplification, but it points to an important fact about *Hamlet* (and fictional art in general). We don't have to believe in ghosts, in revenge, in blood and cruelty, to be able to respond to a work of art. There is a world of difference between the simple, crude depiction of violence (as in the current spate of video films) and the dramatisation of these elements in an aesthetically purposeful manner. The conventions of eighteenth-century French drama did not enable Voltaire and Ducis and Linguet to respond to Shakespeare's *Hamlet*, so that to them it was savage, barbarous. Modern critics as great as T. S. Eliot have been disturbed that the play did not provide 'a set of objects, a situation, a chain of events which shall be the formula' to express the particular emotions dramatised in the play 'in the form of art'. Hence the very proper question asked by Patrick Cruttwell: 'Was Hamlet a good man or was he a bad man?'. After all, a saintly disposition sits ill on a character who kills a counsellor in error, sends two false friends to less-than-richly-deserved deaths, and drives his beloved insane – all with little remorse.

If this were all there were to the play – a chain of violent acts – *Hamlet* could not have attained the success, the *mystique*, it has. It may have begun life at the Universities of Oxford and Cambridge or, at least, have been played there early in its life. (Did the actor who played Polonius go out of his way to win laughs from the student audience by aping someone who had recently acted the part of Julius Caesar in a university play, such as the Latin *Caesar Interfectus*, performed at Christ Church, Oxford, 1582? [See III ii 108–15].) It may be that a shortened and slightly re-arranged version was played at the Globe from that given at the universities, though uncertainties abound when trying to decide the relationship and order of composition of the different versions of Shakespeare's own time. The play has survived countless adaptations, including Garrick's on Voltairean lines in 1772 (discussed later), the *'Naked' Hamlet* produced by Joseph Papp in Central Park, New York in 1968, and Charles Marowitz's *Collage Hamlet* (also discussed later). How can *Hamlet* prove so variously attractive?

The answer stems from two of its outstanding characteristics. The first was noted by Samuel Johnson in 1765. The particular excellence which distinguishes *Hamlet*, he said, was its 'variety'. S. L. Bethell, in a seminal book for our time (*Shakespeare and the Popular Dramatic Tradition*, 1944), took this further: '*Hamlet*, despite notorious complications in the Prince himself, is much more a variety show than the later tragedies'; and Charles Marowitz went further still: 'The comedy of Hamlet' (=*Hamlet*?) 'is imbued with music-hall.' Such variousness – murder and music hall – can clearly offer different kinds of appeal, but integrating such diverse and conflicting elements must have presented Shakespeare with problems in constructing his play and this still presents actors, producers and readers with difficulties. Not surprisingly, as Johnson succinctly put it, 'The conduct [of the play] is not wholly secure against objections'.

That leads to the second great attraction of the play: its mystery. Not for nothing was it numbered amongst the Problem Plays when that term was first concocted by F. S. Boas at the end of the nineteenth century. The mystery, rather than the problem, is of two kinds: the nature of Hamlet the Prince, and how the conflicting elements can be related to make a dramatic whole. Both problems are present together on occasion: Hamlet's behaviour after he has murdered Polonius – especially iv iii, for example – and his exchanges with the Gravediggers and with Osric, juxtaposed about Ophelia's burial and Laertes's distress. Significantly, comedy is present on both occasions, black humour, a cross-talk act (with Hamlet as the 'feed'), and courtly wit. Comedy in *The Tragical History of Hamlet, Prince of Denmark*, as the play was called when first published, is something that demands special attention.

The mysteriousness of *Hamlet*'s attraction can be pinpointed in another way. It is a play about death. What is more, it is a play about youth attempting to grapple with the sense of mortality. The play's – Shakespeare's – most famous speech is not only remarkable for its language. After all, it begins with the very simplest of words: 'To be, or not to be – that is the question', and it comes to the point with chilling simplicity: 'To die, to sleep – no more.' The bleakness of 'No more' is only slightly relieved when, four lines later, the phrases are repeated but followed this time by 'perchance to dream' [III i 56, 60–61, 64–5]. The *fact* of mortality and of corruption, moral and physical, are pervasive in *Hamlet*. The Ghost, that uncertain reality, perhaps mere figment of imagination, is yet, as Maynard Mack puts it, 'the supreme reality . . . witnessing from beyond the grave against this hollow world'. How can such a play *amuse*? *Hamlet*, G. H. Lewes pointed out in 1855, '*amuses* thousands annually', and the italics are his. It is, he said, 'always and everywhere attractive. The lowest and most ignorant audiences delight in it.' Note 'amuses', 'delight', 'attractive'. What in *Hamlet* cannot be fully understood can yet be felt, even by 'the dullest soul' and there is also, he said, 'its wondrous dramatic variety'. Closer to our own time, S. L. Bethell wrote that its popularity in the theatre was due to sheer 'entertainment value'.

So, although Voltaire denounced its barbarity and T. S. Eliot thought the play an artistic failure, its variety and inexplicability, its power to amuse while putting us in seeming touch with that which is beyond knowing, make it ever problematic for producers, actors and audiences. Dover Wilson once aptly remarked that 'it is doubtful whether anyone even in Shakespeare's day ever got to the bottom of everything Hamlet says', and we should rest content with incomplete understanding. Shakespeare himself put it more profoundly. We can apply to *Hamlet* words Shakespeare gives Lafeu in *All's Well that Ends Well*:

> They say miracles are past: and we have our philosophical persons to make modern and familiar, things supernatural and causeless. Hence is it that we make trifles of terrors, ensconcing ourselves into seeming knowledge, when we should submit ourselves to an unknown fear.   [II iii 1–6]

An audience to *Hamlet* submits itself to that unknown fear

whilst simultaneously being entertained, even amused. It is with this paradox that we must come to terms.

The Elusive Text

No play of Shakespeare's presents the editor who must prepare a text for actor or reader with greater problems. The play was first published in 1603 in a pirated version in just the manner that video tapes are pirated nowadays, inferior in content and designed to undercut the legitimate market. Within a year or so a more respectable version, probably deriving from Shakespeare's final but rough draft, was legitimately published and was several times reprinted. Some years after Shakespeare's death in 1616 a third version appeared as part of the Complete Works, the First Folio of 1623. The relationship of these versions is very complicated and every modern edition differs. Look at this innocuous passage at IV ii 17–18 in the text available to you. These are just five possibilities:

1. *Variorum 1877:* he keeps them, like an ape doth nuts, in the corner of his jaw;
2. *Penguin 1937:* He keeps them like an ape in the corner of his jaw,
3. *Norton 1963:* He keeps them like an apple in the corner of his jaw,
4. *New Penguin 1980:* He keeps them, like an ape an apple, in the corner of his jaw,
5. *New Arden 1982:* he keeps them, like an ape, in the corner of his jaw –

The very first edition of *Hamlet* (1603) has 'as an Ape doth nuttes'; the second edition of 1604–5 has 'like an apple'; and the First Folio has 'like an ape'. The 'created' version, 'like an ape an apple', goes back to the late eighteenth century and is to be found also in Professor Alexander's 1951 one-volume edition and the American one-volume Riverside edition of 1974. Ironically, if you went to the Royal Shakespeare Company's production in 1980 and 1981, though that used the New Penguin edition, especially as the basis for its approach to the production (see p. 70 below), you would not have heard any of these words: they were omitted.

That 1603 text is much shorter than those of 1604–5 and 1623. It seems to be an adaptation, just possibly by Shakespeare himself (see p. 43 below), and it indicates that even in Shakespeare's own day, in his own company, cutting and adapting were regarded as legitimate. We should be chary of condemning out of hand those who modify even the plays of Shakespeare; it was a practice recognised in his own day and not only for *Hamlet*.

The most common changes for *Hamlet* are cuts, and these can be extensive. A complete *Hamlet* is a rarity, though Peter Hall – who directed the 1965 *Hamlet* discussed later – did present a complete version at the National Theatre in 1976.

Why cut *Hamlet*? It is Shakespeare's longest play in its number of lines – twice as long as *The Comedy of Errors* – but because of its very variety (for example, a dumb show, a play-within-a-play, songs, a fencing match), it is even longer than the lines themselves indicate. It is a mundane fact that audiences have to be able to catch the last train or bus home. How many a performance has been ruined for those who stay on, as for those who leave early, because of the clatter made by a departing audience in the middle of the fifth act? Gielgud was very conscious of running time for this reason. Very early in the rehearsal of his 1964 New York production he asked:

> How was our timing, by the way? Thirty-six minutes? Well, it will probably take about forty-five. So, counting yesterday, we are up to two hours and fifteen minutes. We have to be careful so that we give them time to catch their trains.

Although we cannot know how effective their regulations were, the authorities of Shakespeare's time required performances (given in the afternoon at theatres such as the Globe) to be terminated in time for the audience to be able to walk home in daylight. That would not give too much time when the days were short in winter.

As even in Shakespeare's own day *Hamlet* seems to have been shortened, it is the more surprising (practical businessman as well as very busy dramatist that he was, writing about two plays a year), that he should not only write at such length but that in the fifth act he should introduce two comic scenes with three completely new comic characters. They can easily be omitted, as Garrick and Marowitz show, but their presence must be indicative of Shakespeare's purpose in some very special way given these circumstances. Modern directors don't usually eliminate Osric and the Gravediggers, though they may cut their lines. The 1965 RSC production cut over 700 lines, between 15 and 20 per cent of the whole play (see Part Two, 9).

In addition to cutting, words may be changed. If editors have difficulty in deciding what *is* the text, it is not surprising that directors should feel free to select from what is available from different versions. Thus the earlier two of the five editions listed above have the famous phrase 'the cease of majesty' (title of a book by M. M. Rees) at III iii 15; the later three have 'cess'; 'cease' derives from the Folio and 'cess' from the 1604–5 text. When he was rehearsing his 1964 production, Gielgud interrupted an early read-through with: 'Guildenstern, can you find some other word for "cess of majesty"? I don't want the audience to spend the next four lines worrying about what it means. I think "cease of majesty" would be better.' The RSC omitted the whole phrase and the next seven lines in 1965; in 1980 the phrase was retained but 'cess', which stood in the text used (the New Penguin) was changed to 'cease'.

Now, such changes may make little difference to anyone but purists; and even academics, though they would select an obscure word for an edition if they believed it to be correct, would understand Gielgud's reasoning and accept the exigencies of theatrical practice. But sometimes the conflict of texts is sharper. Cutting lines can effect characterisation (see p. 72 below) and slight differences between texts can have surprisingly profound ramifications.

To leap or not to leap?

Most, but not all, modern texts have no stage direction for Hamlet at v i 254. That old school warhorse, A. W. Verity's edition of 1911, the Penguin of 1937, and the Complete Pelican Shakespeare (the 'American' Penguin) of 1969 insert after

Hamlet's 'This is I, / Hamlet the Dane', *Hamlet leaps in after Laertes*, or words to that effect. Granville-Barker among others argued that this makes Hamlet the aggressor at this point instead of Laertes. Thus, not only does this direction affect the specific stage action but it also affects the way the actor will interpret the character of Hamlet. That has deeper implications. Is Hamlet here restored to something like normality? Is he now, in v i, to be seen as rational, balanced, having come to terms with mortality and corruption (as suggested by the scene with the Gravediggers, and hence its insertion)? Is there a contrast to be made with Laertes whose emotional excess reminds us, and Hamlet himself, of how Hamlet was before his abortive journey to England? In the next scene Hamlet will not only express his regret at the way he has behaved towards Laertes (a sure sign that he is now rational and generous-minded) but he refers directly to the way Laertes has become, like Hamlet, a revenger:

> But I am very sorry, good Horatio,
> That to Laertes I forgot myself.
> For by the image of my cause I see
> The portraiture of his. I'll court his favours.
> But sure the bravery of his grief did put me
> Into a towering passion.   [v ii 75–80]

In Olivier's film version and in the RSC 1965 and 1980 productions there was no leaping into the grave by Hamlet. Sir John Gielgud, writing on 'The Hamlet Tradition' as an afterpiece to Rosamond Gilder's account of his *Hamlet* of 1934, sees the problem in more practical terms:

> Hamlet and Laertes should surely not fight in the grave, for the moment they disappear from view it is impossible to see clearly what is happening, and the effect on the stage is bound to be ridiculous when they are separated and have to climb sheepishly out again. The lines do not really demand it anyway.*

*Sir John wittily recalls an earlier German production in which *Hamlet* was directed by Reinhardt and played by one of the most famous German actors, Moissi. Ophelia was carried on in white robes on an open bier. There was no trap to represent a grave and so no one leapt in; 'having set the bier above the grave, the men fought over her and were parted, the court retired, and poor Ophelia was left out all night for the daws to peck at, which seemed a little unchristian, to say the least of it'.

By the lines not demanding it, Gielgud doubtless meant the words spoken. Upon what grounds might Hamlet leap into the grave? The source for this stage business is that very first edition of 1603, which gives the direction 'Hamlet leapes in after Laertes'. Now this is a corrupt text and might well be ignored but for a curious fact. The actor who first played Hamlet was Richard Burbage, the company's leading actor and evidently a good friend of Shakespeare's. There is independent evidence from an elegy published shortly after Burbage's death in 1619 that he *did* leap into the grave after Laertes.

> He's gone, and with him what a world are dead,
> Friends, every one, and what a blank instead;
> Take him for all in all he was a man
> Not to be matched, and no age ever can.
> No more young Hamlet, though but scant of breath,
> Shall cry 'Revenge!' for his dear father's death.
> . . .
> Oft have I seen him leap into the grave,
> Suiting the person, which he seemed to have,
> Of a mad lover, with so true an eye,
> That there I would have sworn he meant to die.

Notice, incidentally, how the elegy picks up lines from the play (for example, I ii 187 and v ii 281) and notice how Burbage is described as acting, *becoming* the character he acts, something vouched for by a slightly later writer, Richard Flecknoe in 1664. Burbage, he says, 'was a delightful Proteus, so wholly transforming himself into his part, and putting off himself with his clothes, as he never (not so much as in the Tiring-house) assumed himself again until the play was done'. Nowadays this is a norm, but we can see the tradition of the actor becoming the part he played going way back beyond Stanislavsky in Burbage and disseminated on the Continent by David Garrick who impressed eighteenth-century French writers and critics with his ability to become the roles he played. Hence Olivier's aim: 'I wanted audiences seeing the film to say, not, "There is Laurence Olivier dressed like Hamlet", but "That is Hamlet".'

What that direction in the 1603 edition indicates, therefore, is that Burbage, the first Hamlet, *did* leap into the grave and

was especially remembered for it. What then is our authority?
What gets into print – a hitty-missy business in Shakespeare's
day, or what we know to have been performed by Shakespeare's
own company? *Hamlet*'s variety extends beyond character,
diverse elements, and implications: there is variety between the
texts and traditions of performance, each with some claim to
'authority'.

In one version selected here for discussion, Hamlet *does* leap
into the grave. Ironically, this is the New York production
directed by Gielgud who, thirty years earlier, had found no
support for this in the lines. Again in rehearsal he appealed to
the text:

> *Burton (Hesitating)* John, you don't think we could fight outside
> the grave? There's such a danger of being comic.
> *Gielgud* No. Hamlet is competing with Laertes. It's in the text
> and the lines require it. Try it again.

Eventually 'Burton did an exciting leap from the platform into
the grave which both he and Gielgud thought worked well',
according to Sterne; but the filmed stage-play shows only a
fairly modest stride over a table turned on its side to represent a
grave.

John Gielgud's sensitivity to Shakespeare is rightly famous.
That he has interpreted this little moment on the authority of
'the lines' so differently points to an uncertainty inherent in the
text itself and, beyond that, to the mystery at the heart of
Hamlet.

2   THE CHARACTER OF HAMLET

The peculiar character of Hamlet 'provides a fascinating subject for every variety of arm-chair quackery', asserts S. L.
Bethell with feeling and some truth. Hamlet's peculiar fascina-
tion may stem partly from some innate mystery, a mysteriousness into which he himself delves as he seeks to tease out his

motives and responses; partly from his capacity to strike a chord of fellow-feeling in so many audiences over the centuries: 'It is *we* who are Hamlet', said Hazlitt in 1817; and partly, it must be admitted, to the imperfections in Shakespeare's character-drawing. We are sometimes unsure whether our uncertainty and Hamlet's mystery stem from the exactness or the imprecision of the dramatisation. Thus Hamlet's contradictory assertions to Ophelia 'I did love you once' and 'I loved you not' [III i 115, 119] and the contrast between his treatment of Ophelia and his claim to Laertes, 'I loved Ophelia' [v i 265]. The line just quoted from Bethell is preceded by one arguing that the play is 'a favourite with the critics because its imperfections leave more room for discussion'. The most recent editor of *Hamlet*, Professor Harold Jenkins, puts the problem succinctly: 'audiences, and still more readers, have looked for a kind of consistency Shakespeare does not always bother to supply'.

The reverse of the complications of armchair quackery is the simply bold statement about Hamlet. Olivier, after the Prologue he reads to begin his film version [from I iv 23–36], offers one such. In measured tones he explains: 'This is the tragedy of a man who could not make up his mind.' This might half-convince us did not Olivier's film suggest much more. Charles Marowitz likens Hamlet to many contemporary intellectuals who equate 'taking up a position with the performance of an action' – those who believe that 'by trumpeting their moral righteousness to the world they are actively remedying a situation'. Again, some truth; but, though I know many such academics, I know only one Hamlet and he is like none of them.

The simple question that Patrick Cruttwell poses, already mentioned, focuses on the complexities of Hamlet, character and play: 'Was Hamlet a good man or was he a bad one?' If Hamlet *is* mad, then much of what he does may be excused. However, attitudes to madness have changed; we are more sensitive to its depiction than is suggested by Shakespeare's phrase 'an antic disposition' [I v 172], or Samuel Johnson's finding cause for 'much mirth' in Hamlet's pretended madness. Actors are less willing, it would seem, to present a thoroughly distracted Hamlet (though that does not apply to enactments of Ophelia). Thus we have the paradox of, at most, a slightly neurotic Prince driving Ophelia to mental breakdown. If Hamlet is sane and his madness 'mere policy', can he be 'good'?

One way out, as Cruttwell explains, is to take account of the circumstances in which Hamlet finds himself. The play is not simply a projection of Hamlet's mind (though, for his *Collage* version, Marowitz sees the events and characters of the play as figments of Hamlet's imagination, after the manner of Arthur Miller's *Death of a Salesman*, originally called *The Inside of His Head*). *Hamlet* can be said to have two quite distinct kinds of location. It takes place at Elsinore at a court that is corrupt, at least as interpreted by Hamlet; it is presided over by a king who has incestuously married Hamlet's mother. Hamlet has every reason to be appalled, disgusted, even shamed. His turning against Ophelia, if not an instance of his irrationality, real or feigned (and if the madness is feigned, nothing is better contrived than his cruelty to Ophelia to persuade the court that his mind is disturbed), can be seen as the transfer to Ophelia of the disgust he feels towards his mother. Not surprisingly, Hamlet turns that disgust inwards on himself— see especially 'O, what a rogue and peasant slave am I!' [ii ii 547–603]. A verse by a little-read nineteenth-century poet, Richard Hengist Horne, sums up the effect very plainly:

> Self-disgust
> Gnaws at the roots of being, and doth hang
> A heavy sickness on the beams of day.
> Cursèd! accursèd be the freaks of nature,
> That mar us from ourselves.

The second 'location' is that of the play's genre. *Hamlet* is a revenge tragedy, a form very popular in its day, which took as its starting point the absolute necessity for personal vengeance denied to the English with the coming to power of the Tudors and their stronger state-enforcement of the rule of law. Hamlet was neither the first nor the last hero bound to exact vengeance as a sort of proxy for something which was now outlawed (compare the vogue for war movies). What is unusual is that this task is laid on one so unfitted to carry it through – unfitted, say, in comparison with Laertes or Fortinbras, who both pursue revenge much more actively [see iv v 133–8 and i i 95–104 respectively]. This is not to say that Hamlet is particularly cowardly (as he himself declares [II ii 568]), or pigeon-livered [II ii 574], or even that he, like Marowitz's intellectual, 'Must like a whore unpack my heart with words' [II ii 583], that is, merely talk about his task. No, it is simply that Hamlet is basically on the side of the angels, educated to think deeply, and is thus genuinely appalled at what the Ghost demands of him. Shakespeare suggests this with remarkable economy, an economy that is possibly so artistically refined that it might be missed or taken for no more than casual interjection. Look at Hamlet's words – they are scarcely speeches – just after the Ghost has told him he is bound to take revenge: 'What?', 'O God!', 'Murder?' [I v 8, 24, 26]. If we do not respond appropriately here, Hamlet's aptness (to use Shakespeare's word) to accept the duty of revenge [I v 29–30] may come too quickly for a twentieth-century mind attuned to psychological realism and unaware of the conventional stereotypes upon which Shakespeare builds. Our difficulty arises in much the same way that difficulties of character interpretation can arise with Shylock and Falstaff. Out of stereotypes (the Revenger, Vice, Usurer or Crabbed Father) Shakespeare creates characters whom we may be forgiven for thinking of as real human beings. Mere convention is in conflict with creative genius.

The circumstances in which Hamlet is placed are made even more complex and uncertain by the Ghost. Although Hamlet assures Horatio and Marcellus that 'It is an honest ghost' [I v 138], he is less certain. When the Ghost leaves he cries on heaven and earth and goes on, 'What else? And shall I couple hell?'. Later, in his 'Rogue and peasant slave' speech it is easy to pass over that same conjunction repeated at line 582: 'Prompted to my revenge by heaven and hell'. At III ii 92 Hamlet explains to Horatio that if the King is unmoved by the play, 'It is a damnèd ghost that we have seen'. It is not just a matter of whether Hamlet is good or bad, but whether the Ghost is good or bad, too. Hamlet's dilemma in this respect would be well understood in Shakespeare's day. Writers such as Lewes Lavater (whose work was translated into English in 1572) wrote not only on whether ghosts might really be seen or not – pointing out that they might be figments of the imagination caused by 'melancholy, madness, weakness of the senses, fear, or some other perturbation' – but also explained that they might be good or bad angels, or souls in heaven, purgatory or hell. Lavater also provided tests by which a good spirit might be distinguished from an evil one. Note how Hamlet questions Horatio about the apparition [I ii 226–42]. The Ghost claims to abide in Purgatory (a trifle odd for a king of a state Protestant in Shakespeare's time), and he passes three of the four tests. The sticking point is whether the Ghost is asking something that 'doth vary from the doctrine of the apostles'. Revenge is outside that doctrine. Once again, Shakespeare provides an unresolved conflict. He writes in the genre of Revenge Tragedy, but the milieu he depicts is clearly Christian, sinful though it be.

Hamlet *must* be seen in the context in which Shakespeare places him, but that context is at odds with itself. It must be admitted that this is a weakness in the play. Curiously, rather than undermining the play, it sorts well with it, almost being tantamount to the dilemma in which the Prince finds himself. The tangle into which Shakespeare has got himself is not unlike the everyday dilemmas we all find difficult to resolve.

Other explanations have been offered to help tease out Hamlet's character. He has been seen as an example of melancholic man and, more recently, explained in Freudian terms as an instance of the Oedipal complex. Freud explained Hamlet's delay by recourse to this theory and, in a famous essay (*Hamlet and Oedipus*, 1949) Ernest Jones made plain how 'the play has appeared to mean something important, though not something easily definable, to a wide variety of men', as Clifford Leech put it. Possibly most helpful is Jones's explanation for Hamlet's harsh treatment of Ophelia. This, says Jones, partly stems from the revulsion he feels for his mother's behaviour (which Hamlet transfers to women in general and Ophelia in particular) and for Ophelia's too-ready acceptance of her father's and brother's attitudes to Hamlet's natural affection.

It is easy for us to misunderstand the word 'melancholy' today. In Elizabethan times the word was related to the theory of the four humours which were thought to control human temperament. Patrick Cruttwell has likened this melancholy to the temperament of the scholar, the meditative man. Hamlet had recently been studying at Wittenberg University (attended by Luther and Marlowe's Dr Faustus) and he intended to return there. Melancholia was, however, fashionable in Shakespeare's time in a way that meditativeness is certainly not today. It could, perhaps, be but a pose. Not long before Shakespeare began writing there was published in London *A Treatise on Melancholy*, written by Timothy Bright. Although some scholars (such as Harold Jenkins) have thought 'the influence of Bright on Shakespeare's conception of Hamlet has been much exaggerated', some of Bright's description, if it does not show influence, reveals a strikingly similar view. According to Bright, in human beings melancholy 'breedeth a jealousy of doubt in that they take in deliberation, and causeth them to be the more exact and curious in pondering the very moments of things. . . . Such persons are doubtful, suspicious, and thereby long in deliberation.' The melancholic's dreams are fearful and (particularly intriguing) his house, 'except it be cheerful and lightsome, trim and neat', seems like a prison or dungeon [see II ii 241–50]. But most significant in the light of our possible misconception of the melancholic as one of a morose and bitter nature, is Bright's assertion that 'Sometime it falleth out that melancholy men are found very witty', as Hamlet assuredly is.

Given Hamlet's nature, and the profound issues of good and evil and life after death raised by the Ghost's demand for revenge, it is hardly surprising that, unlike Fortinbras and Laertes, Hamlet should ponder long and hard on the matter of revenge. Olivier's opening statement, 'This is the tragedy of a man who could not make up his mind' has no more than an element of truth in it. What makes the play especially appealing is all that leads to that delay. Shakespeare has performed the difficult task of dramatising thought rather than action (and that makes special problems for a film director, given that film is, by and large, the medium for action). It so happens that in any reasonable production, delay is not something that strikes us strongly. The issue of delay is for the reader, for the study. In production, with Hamlet bodied out by a real, living person, we are far more conscious of the issues posed by the Ghost's demand.

3   THE COMEDY OF 'HAMLET'

Nowhere is the distinction greater between text and performance than in the matter of comedy. It is not simply that what
makes one person laugh leaves another unmoved, but rather
the difficulties of recognising as comedy what on the printed
page seems uncomic; secondly, imagining the stage business
that makes lines comic; and thirdly, not finding comedy where
none exists. Performance can help enormously, but performance itself depends on the text or upon received tradition; for
this, the passage of time hardly helps.

In the pirated edition of *Hamlet* of 1603, some lines were
added to those written by Shakespeare. Most modern editions
omit these but the New Penguin edition includes them, as
Shakespeare's, at III ii 43–53 (see Commentary, p. 276).
Despite the New Penguin editor's argument, it is more likely
that the actor who first played Hamlet, Richard Burbage, has
himself done what, in the part of Hamlet, he is telling the
clowns not to do: that is, he *ad libs*. As it is most unusual for a
straight actor to *ad lib*, then or now, this looks very much like
Burbage's riposte to his good friend Shakespeare. Because it is
Burbage *ad libbing*, the audience will assume that these are lines
he is supposed to say as part of his role in the play, so that only
members of the company would realise the nature of the 'joke'.
There is nothing a modern performance can do to revivify this
moment. But one can go further.

Hamlet – or Burbage, if this conjecture is correct – tells how
the gentlemen playgoers write down in their notebooks jests of
comedians with a limited repertoire and then call out the
punch-lines before the clown can get to them in his stories. And
he gives examples of these 'jests': 'Cannot you stay till I eat my
porridge?'; 'You owe me a quarter's wages'; 'My coat wants a
cullison', and 'Your beer is sour'. Now, by working very hard
one can raise a slight laugh – a titter as Frankie Howerd would
say – by the time the third or fourth of these is reached, but such
laughter as transpires derives more from the performer's technique than from the lines themselves. One of these catch-
phrases appears in a jest book of the time and also in a single
play (*A Yorkshire Tragedy*, 1606), but even in the context of a play

it would not raise a laugh today. Recognising the comic from the printed page, especially for plays of an early period or different culture, can obviously be very difficult.

Now I have glided over comedy and what rouses laughter as if they were the same, which, of course, they are not. Ben Jonson, Shakespeare's contemporary, went so far as to argue that 'the moving of laughter is a fault in comedy, a kind of turpitude, that depraves some part of a man's nature without a disease'. This may be to take things too far, but it warns usefully against assuming that comedy must automatically be funny and that what is funny is necessarily of the genre, Comedy. This is important to bear in mind when considering comedy and the use of humour in *Hamlet*.

There are other problems. Take, for instance, this little exchange:

GUILD	But we both obey,
	And here give up ourselves in the full bent
	To lay our service freely at your feet,
	To be commanded.
KING	Thanks, Rosencrantz and gentle Guildenstern.
QUEEN	Thanks, Guildenstern and gentle Rosencrantz.

[II ii 29–33]

Rarely, if ever, do commentators say anything about this passage in editions of the play; its meaning, so far as the words go, is plain enough. But is it meant to raise a laugh, as it has on occasion at Stratford? How is it to be performed? Richard David, contrasting the National Theatre production of 1976 with that at the Roundhouse in the same year, remarked (referring first to the National):

Rosencrantz and Guildenstern, constantly sweeping off their hats in an exaggerated unison to signify their compliance with Claudius's commands, become a pair of faceless automatons very different from the subtly diversified and ten times more dangerous false friends at the Roundhouse. And we were treated again to the corny old joke of making the Queen's repetition of Claudius's acknowledgment – 'Thanks, Rosencrantz and gentle Guildenstern' – with the names reversed, a correction, with the suggestion that the two were so indistinguishable that the King has mistaken one

for the other. At the Roundhouse, King and Queen were in full
agreement as to the identities of their guests, and Gertrude's rever-
sal of the names was merely an elegant courtesy to ensure that each
was accorded equal precedence.

Two totally different ways of interpreting these innocuous-
seeming lines. (Although the Gielgud/Burton production did
not strive for a laugh here, one was to be heard from the theatre
audience of the filmed stage-play.) Note also the different effect
of meaning in its broader, not merely verbal sense, of Rosencrantz and Guildenstern's business with their hats.

The treatment of the Ghost raises rather trickier problems.
There is no doubt that the Ghost ought to thrill even a blasé,
sophisticated modern audience. Often it doesn't; the key to
doing so may be found in something Charles Marowitz wrote in
the Introduction to his *Collage Hamlet*: 'What is frightening
about a ghost is not its unearthliness, but its earthliness: its
semblance of reality divorced from existence.' Given that this
is successfully achieved (and note how the RSC's Ghost in 1965
was much larger than life-size), what is one to make of the
swearing to silence sequence in I v?

Hamlet insists that Marcellus and Horatio swear that they
will not reveal what they have seen that night. He demands
they swear upon his sword. It is worth noting in passing that in
performance the physical nature of the sword can give force to
its dual imagery. It is at once a warlike object, in its way
representative of the war background to the play (the very
'source of this our watch' being Fortinbras's 'post haste and
romage in the land' [I i 106–7]), and its hilt forms a crucifix upon
which they will swear and which is used to dramatic effect in
this manner at other points in the play (see below, p. 71, for
David Warner's 'business' with the sword as crucifix at the
beginning of IV ii and Plate 5). In this way the 'necessary
business' of the play in performance can fruitfully bring out the
essential ambiguities of the language. Thus in Hamlet's
urgency with Horatio and Marcellus:

HAM.	Never make known what you have seen tonight.
HOR. & MAR.	My lord, we will not.
HAM.	Nay, but swear't.

HOR.	In faith,
	My lord, not I.
MAR.	Nor I, my lord – in faith.
HAM.	Upon my sword.
MAR.	We have sworn, my lord, already.
HAM.	Indeed, upon my sword, indeed. [i v 144–8]

There are three, possibly four, stages to this brief dialogue.
First, Horatio and Marcellus promise not to reveal what they
have seen [145]; Hamlet then demands they swear to that,
which they do, Marcellus repeating Horatio's 'in faith' almost
as an afterthought so that the everyday 'i'faith' becomes what it
originally was, an attestation of faith. This is still not enough for
Hamlet: they must, in the third stage, swear upon his sword.
Now if the sword is presented blade first, his demand carries
with it an element of threat. Marcellus protests they have
already sworn [147]. Hamlet's reply repeats the word 'indeed'
(in contrast to his companions' use of 'in faith'). How is this
said? Threateningly? More significantly, what business
accompanies this line? If Hamlet were, as a fourth stage in this
short sequence, to reverse his sword on this line, presenting the
hilt, with its religious implications foremost in sight and mind,
the whole tenor of the incident would change direction.

But now there is a further change of tone. What follows has
all the potentialities for *low* comedy, almost burlesque – of
which Burton made the most, and to which the audience
responded with loud laughter.

        The Ghost cries under the stage

GHOST	Swear.
HAM.	Ha, ha, boy, sayst thou so? Art thou there, truepenny?
	Come on. You hear this fellow in the cellarage.
	Consent to swear.
	. . .
GHOST	*(beneath)* Swear
HAM.	*Hic et ubique?* Then we'll shift our ground.
	. . .
GHOST	*(beneath)* Swear by his sword.
HAM.	Well said, old mole! Canst work i'th'earth so fast?
	A worthy pioneer! Once more remove, good friends.
HOR.	O day and night, but this is wondrous strange!
	[i v 149–52, 155–6, 161–4]

At least three characteristics of this passage require comment: the stage movement necessitated by the words and its effect; Hamlet's badinage; and the significance of certain words.

The Ghost certainly strikes apprehension in Hamlet's colleagues; e.g. Barnardo's

> How now, Horatio? You tremble and look pale.
> Is not this something more than fantasy?   [I i 53–4]

To critics such as Maynard Mack, 'the ghost is the supreme reality, representative of the hidden ultimate power, in Bradley's terms – witnessing from beyond the grave against this hollow world'. To producers such as Peter Hall in 1965, the Ghost assumed superhuman proportions, standing from 8 to 12 feet high depending which theatre critic one read. It was big enough to require a trolley to move it and a double so that rapid exits and entrances could be made at opposite sides of the stage. Gielgud's Ghost in 1964 was inspired by the words 'Stay, illusion' [I i 128]. The audience saw only a huge shadow of a helmeted head with shoulders, supposedly cast by a figure off-stage, and heard Gielgud's recorded voice, at first husky but gradually becoming less so. The actors addressed the figure supposedly off-stage, the shadow being behind them. However, as the shadow was actually cast by a projector also behind the actors, and as a pillar stood between the actors and the screen, part of this 'shadow' was illogically obscured at times. And, surely, ghosts do not cast shadows!

Hamlet's jocular familiarity with the Ghost – 'truepenny', 'this fellow in the cellarage', *'Hic et ubique?'* (Here and everywhere?), 'old mole', 'worthy pioneer' – contrast strangely with a figure representative of 'supreme reality' and so fearsome to Hamlet's friends. It may be that he is anxious to disguise from his colleagues just how seriously he takes the Ghost's behests, but this explanation needs to be considered in the context of the stage movements. Those movements are demanded by the language as those on-stage seek to locate the old mole who can tunnel through the earth so fast. The movements of Horatio and Marcellus may represent their fear as they seek to escape the Ghost; or it may be in response to the Ghost's demands so that they make their oaths above the position whence he intones

'Swear'. How this is realised in performance depends upon the director's understanding. The voice of the Ghost is often artificially modified to make it more sepulchral. The total effect is – or should be – a curious combination of the fearsome and the comic.

The scene can be played wholly seriously, but that is to miss an essential element. Olivier achieved this in the film by cutting out virtually the whole of this section, having his Ghost utter 'Swear' only once. Certainly the scene should not slip into burlesque. Both the comic and the fearful were achieved in the 1976 Roundhouse production, according to Richard David. Delicate control ensured that the 'farcical extravagance aggravated by the marvellous adroitness with which the "old mole" was made to move underground, never got out of hand'. Helen Gardner once brought out the relationship between the fearful and the comic by a very neat modern parallel. She pointed out that Reilly, the all-knowing psychiatrist in T. S. Eliot's *The Cocktail Party*, is also treated ambiguously. Eliot, she explains, 'has been able to exploit for comic purposes our ambivalent feelings about "mind doctors" '. We have no difficulty in seeing psychiatrists simultaneously as a power, a threat, and comically; so is the Ghost in I v. Those conflicts of modes were as 'normal' to an Elizabethan audience as those exploited by T. S. Eliot in our day.

This tonal ambiguity matches to perfection – or rather, realises dramatically in performance – the uncertainties attendant on the Ghost for Hamlet and us. Shakespeare keeps prompting our uncertainty by his choice of words and his requirements for stage movement. It should also be noted that Hamlet is *already* acceding to one of the Ghost's demands: making Horatio and Marcellus swear secrecy. Hamlet says the Ghost is honest, but it is heard under the stage (in the cellarage) – and 'under the stage' was the location of hell in the Elizabethan theatre. The early stage directions specifically require that the Ghost cry from under the stage. 'Old mole' might be a nickname for the devil; 'pioneer' (or a sapper) was certainly used for devils who travelled through the earth. And a devil is by no stretch of imagination 'honest'. Thus do tonal and verbal uncertainties reflect the duality of the stage movement. This conflict of tones in I v is to be found throughout the play,

for example in Hamlet's behaviour towards Ophelia at the play
[III ii 121–44, 254–61] – see p. 63 below for Alec Guinness's stage
business here – and in his response to questions asking the
whereabouts of Polonius after he has murdered him [IV iii
16–30].

English drama since the Middle Ages has notoriously defied
conventions of dramatic decorum so generally accepted on the
Continent, especially those that insist upon the separation of
the comic and the tragic. Thus, in certain medieval cycles of
plays telling the story of Christian salvation, notably those
associated with Wakefield and York, even the Crucifixion of
Christ is presented in a context of rough humour. Paradoxically, in a more secular age we may find it difficult to laugh at a
scene of such cruelty, but in its own day an audience would
have been able to respond simultaneously to the suffering and
the comedy. The function of such comedy was to draw the
audience's laughter and thus to place each spectator on the side
of the torturers or knights crucifying Christ. Thus those watching the spectacle, if tempted to laugh, become as guilty as those
perpetrating the act. This use of comedy still flourished in
Shakespeare's day. The religious cycles did not die out, as some
drama histories suggest, but were stopped forcibly by Queen
Elizabeth's government because of their association with 'the
old faith', Roman Catholicism. By a strange coincidence, the
year the first professional theatre was built in London (when
Shakespeare was twelve years old) saw the imprisonment in the
Tower of the authorities who had permitted such a cycle to be
performed at Chester. Shakespeare and his contemporaries,
and their audiences, were capable of responding simultaneously to the comic and that which aroused pain (that is, to the
pathetic, from the Greek *páthos*, suffering).

In recent years, with the advent of Arden, Beckett, Orton,
Osborne and Pinter, something of that capacity has been
restored to us and companies such as the RSC and the National
have been adept at realising this conflict of emotions in performance. Anthony Sher's Fool in the RSC 1982 *King Lear* is a
notable example. What seemed to Voltaire to be vulgar and
barbarous has been rediscovered for what it was originally
intended to be: a dramatisation of the essential conflict of
emotions and forces within us which demands of us a judge-

ment. To oversimplify very considerably, we judge through the correctness of our responses (for example, when and what to laugh at), whether, in Lafeu's words, we are making 'trifles of terrors, ensconcing ourselves into seeming knowledge' when we should instead be submitting to 'an unknown fear'.

Hamlet uses comedy in a masterly way in direct line with that medieval tradition. This is particularly to be seen in the use of *comédie noire* (a term derived from Anouilh's plays of the 1930s and 1940s): that grotesquerie found in I v, III ii, IV iii, and the scene between Hamlet and the Gravedigger in v i. The humour of *Hamlet* is much more varied than this, however. There are at least three characters who could be classed as comics, especially were the play not a tragedy: Polonius, Osric and the First Gravedigger. Polonius is not the fool that Osric is, and some productions present him seriously or (as did Peter Hall) show his fooling as a mask to his political cunning. All, however, are focal points of comedy. Osric's play with his hat (and in some productions, that of Rosencrantz and Guildenstern: see above, p. 25) would not be out of place in a modern pantomime. (It was particularly noticeable in the Gielgud/Burton modern rehearsal-dress production that Osric, exceptionally, had a showy, befeathered hat to flourish.) There is repartee [II ii 206–9, 213–15], music-hall cross-talk comedy [v i 120–7]; riddles and conundrums [v i 41–59, 127–34]; clowning (obviously Osric and the Gravediggers, but note also Hamlet's forcing of a recorder upon Guildenstern [III ii 353–79] and, of course, his advice to the clowns [III ii 37–43]); irony (a nice example being Hamlet's 'Thrift, thrift, Horatio. The funeral baked meats / Did coldly furnish forth the marriage tables' [I ii 180–1]: Burton got a good laugh on 'Thrift, thrift'); bawdy (especially and paradoxically in the scenes with Ophelia); the absurd (Polonius's 'pastoral-comical' speech [II ii 395–401, and his conversation with Hamlet about the shapes of clouds [III ii 383–90]); and, inevitably, much wordplay, two examples of which must suffice: 'A little more than kin, and less than kind!' [I ii 65]; and 'Conception is a blessing. But as your daughter may conceive . . .' [II ii 184–5]. Quite often the humour is used in a way wholly appropriate to comedy. This is particularly apparent in the Polonius, Osric and Gravedigger scenes; but even such a line as 'A little more than kin, and less than kind' has to be spoken as an aside: the device as typical of comedy as the soliloquy is of tragedy. The aside prompts an intimate relationship between character and audience; our support is actively solicited. Thus we are prompted to see things from Hamlet's point of view and must be alive to judging whether we always agree with that.

Just as there are many kinds of humour, so does it perform many functions in the play. The biting satire scourges – such satire was then much in fashion; its apparent misplacement (in the Ghost and Ophelia scenes) may prompt unease and uncertainty in us; it counterbalances to some extent the brooding on death; in Act v the comedy is a means for dramatising a rejuvenated Hamlet come to terms with obsessive thoughts of mortality, rather than – as the famous eighteenth-century editor, Steevens, described this element in a letter to David Garrick – a farce entitled 'The Gravediggers; with the pleasant humours of Osric, the Danish Macaroni'. (Steevens in his edition, 1778, also considered that Hamlet killed the King to revenge himself, not his father.)

If Polonius, Osric and the First Gravedigger are focal points of comedy, it is nevertheless Hamlet who is always involved in humour of every kind. For a character whom we take to be so brooding, so introspective, as black as the clothes he traditionally wears, this is remarkable. It is not simply to be explained by Timothy Bright's association of wit with melancholy (see the earlier discussion, above). Hamlet's humour is properly to be termed wit, and that word 'wit' should be considered not solely as a word for a kind of comedy but as retaining something of its original Anglo-Saxon meaning: 'intelligence', from the verb, *witan*, 'to know'. Hamlet's wit is a mark of his intellectual superiority. His very university, perhaps fortuitously, implies the same idea – Wittenberg. Hamlet's wit, his power of mind, takes expression in both his attempt to puzzle out the meaning of life and death, and in his humour.

Getting a grasp of the humour of the play (and, for a tragedy, it is often a very funny play) is therefore especially important for any production. Humour is a determinant of Hamlet's nature and a key to the tonal quality of the play as a whole. As so many of the characters are a source, or a focus, of comedy, it is noticeable that this does not apply to Claudius and Gertrude.

Hamlet, especially through its use of comedy, demands that an audience make judgements and ensures that it 'thinks through the skin', as it were, so uniting feeling and thought. This is one reason for the play's sustained power over centuries and across cultures. It is not possible to understand *Hamlet*, nor present it adequately on the stage, without coming to terms with the comedy. Vivian Mercier, writing of Samuel Beckett's drama, distinguished two kinds of humour: the macabre, and the grotesque. 'Oversimplifying', he said, 'these two types of humour help us to accept death and to belittle life.' That might well be applied to the use of humour in *Hamlet*.

4 Speeches, Choral and in Character

That we can read, indeed study, a play by Shakespeare without ever seeing it, is for the obvious reason that it is made up at one level of words, words arranged as dialogue and as 'speeches'. The proportion of stage directions to words spoken – even in a modern edition of Shakespeare, which will have considerably amplified the directions – is very small. So important are the words in a play by Shakespeare that some critics have, mistakenly, read the plays as if they were poems. That they can be so read at all is one mark of Shakespeare's genius, but it gives limited understanding. And to reverse the process and imagine the words are but the small change of television soap-opera is as absurd. What is said here should be read in conjunction with later discussions of how words are said, especially Burton's delivery of the 'Rogue and peasant slave' speech (see Part Two, 8).

Shakespeare invests his words with a depth and richness that repay precisely the kind of attention we give complex poetry. Plays and characters' speeches will be marked by a preponderance of certain kinds of imagery. Thus, Caroline Spurgeon in her study, *Leading Motives in the Imagery of Shakespeare's Tragedies* (1930), suggested that the dominating image representative of the unwholesome moral condition of Denmark is that of an ulcer or tumour. The atmosphere of the play is due in part, she argues, 'to the number of images of sickness, disease, or blemish of the body'. She goes on to argue that to Shakespeare's 'pictorial imagination' the problem posed by the play is not that of a mind 'too philosophic or a nature temperamentally unfitted to act quickly', but 'something greater and even more mysterious, being rather that condition of life itself for which the individual is not himself to blame', any more than 'the sick man is to blame for the cancer which strikes and devours him'.

Although non-verbal means can provide basic information, sketch character and rouse emotions, much of what we hear in Shakespeare sets the scene, tells the story and expresses character. In the first scene of *Hamlet* we are not only told of the Ghost's visitation but the fact that Denmark is on a war footing for fear of Fortinbras. Basically this is exposition, setting the scene. At every point we learn something else: that it is bitterly cold; that there are different interpretations of ghosts ('Horatio says 'tis but our fantasy', line 23); that despite the irreligious demand for vengeance, this is a society recognising 'our Saviour's birth' (160); and so on.

Much of the immediate dramatic tension in any play is derived from the interchange of language between characters. In this short exchange there is both the passing of information, comedy, and a heightening of tension:

KING   Where is Polonius?
HAMLET   In heaven. Send thither to see. If your messenger find him not there, seek him i'th'other place yourself. But if indeed you find him not within this month, you shall nose him as you go up the stairs into the lobby.
KING   *(to attendants)* Go seek him there.
HAMLET   'A will stay till you come.   *Exeunt attendants.*
                                                        [IV iii 31–8]

Hamlet does say where Polonius is to be found, but he also insults the King by suggesting he would appropriately be his own messenger to hell. The black comedy of ' 'A will stay till you come' may elicit a laugh from us, but as we laugh we might well check our response; we are laughing at murder, and as such become, as it were, Hamlet's accomplice. We don't think out these possibilities as we hear these few lines in performance, but that is the kind of response which even such a seemingly simple exchange can prompt.

A characteristic of tragedies of Shakespeare's time was the soliloquy. Hamlet explains his dilemma in a series of soliloquies and it is not unusual to consider these as a related sequence: 'O that this too too sullied flesh would melt' [I ii 129–59]; 'O, what a rogue and peasant slave am I!' [II ii 547–603] and 'How all occasions do inform against me' [IV iv 32–66]. To these should be added 'To be, or not to be' [III i 56–90], which is not strictly a soliloquy as Ophelia is present, and [II ii 293–310], the speech which includes 'What a piece of work is a man'. All are in verse except the last. Analysis of these passages is not the concern here (see, for example, the splendid account of 'To be, or not to be' in the New Arden, pp. 484–93). I propose to contrast one of the soliloquies with a speech which fulfils a totally different function, Gertrude's 'There is a willow grows askant the brook' [IV vii 166–83]. (For the problem of speaking famous speeches on-stage which are well-known out of context, see below, p. 63.)

Although it is conventional to refer to the soliloquy, 'O, what a rogue and peasant slave am I!' as if this were the first line, it is preceded by 'Now I am alone'. Shakespeare may seem to be stressing the obvious, for there is no one else on the stage, but he is pointing up Hamlet's isolation – in spirit rather than physically – that is the tragic hero's peculiar condition. Traditionally in a soliloquy the speaker reveals his true self to the audience. Richard III tells the audience of his plans. Hamlet does the same, though his scheme is less nefarious than Richard's. He also bitterly upbraids himself. He contrasts himself to an actor, someone traditionally able to feign feelings – the Greek word for an actor has become our word 'hypocrite'. The recent RSC production of *Hamlet* takes the theatrical imagery that pervades the play as its starting point (see below, p. 70). Ironically, as Hamlet whips himself into a fury, he acts out his feelings. Few actors have better realised this in performance than Richard Burton, whose recording of this speech, divorced from its context, can still stun the listener (see Part Two, 8). The speech makes links with what has gone before, reviving doubts about the Ghost:

HAM.   . . .   The spirit that I have seen
             May be a devil, and the devil hath power
             T'assume a pleasing shape, yea, and perhaps
             Out of my weakness and my melancholy,
             As he is very potent with such spirits,
             Abuses me to damn me. . . .   [ii ii 596–601]

In Elizabethan English, 'spirit' could mean a devil, as in Marlowe's *Doctor Faustus*, and devils were notorious for their ability
to assume a pleasing shape. Marlowe makes satiric use of this
ability. When Faustus conjures up a devil, he says:

             I charge thee to return and change thy shape.
             Thou art too ugly to attend on me.
             Go, and return an old Franciscan friar:
             That holy shape becomes a devil best.   [*Dr F*. i iii 23–6]

In so far as this speech does not advance the action it may, like
its parallel in iv iv, be considered 'unnecessary'. Even the 'plot'
to present a play is misleading in strictly narrative terms for
Hamlet has already decided on this course of action and has
just asked the First Player to learn a new speech he would insert
(lines 538–9). In his film version, Olivier cuts out all the
soliloquy except 'The play's the thing' passage (see Part Two,
7). Yet, as Olivier was concerned with 'a man who could not
make up his mind', in effect he cut out what in part explained
why Hamlet was as Olivier described him.
    In part, this soliloquy, whilst not acknowledging the audi-
ence's presence* (which always happens in a clown's mono-
logue – a key to understanding the origins of Richard iii in the
Vice), explores Hamlet's self-disgust which sets him apart from
and above the other two revengers: Laertes, whose impetuosity
expresses such insensitivity that he would offer hell allegiance
and dare damnation [iv v 133, 135]; and Fortinbras, who,
though 'a delicate and tender prince' goes to war for 'a little

---

*It was remarked by the theatre critic Alan Brien that David Warner *did* directly
address the audience. His appeals were 'for our support and understanding and
established an intense rapport which is rarely obtained by more fluent and sonorous
Hamlets. It creates an atmosphere almost like a teach-in.' Burton – fluent and sonorous
par excellence – seemed positively to avoid looking in the direction of the audience, and
the effect was quite artificial.

patch of ground / That hath no profit but the name' [IV iv 48, 28–9]. In this soliloquy we see directly into Hamlet's heart and mind and can understand how his hesitation is based on a conclusion he reached when referring to Fortinbras: 'Rightly to be great / Is not to stir without great argument' [IV iv 53–4]. Rather than argue 'no delay, no play,' one might suggest instead that Delay *is* the Play. This soliloquy is one means by which Shakespeare dramatises delay in a narrative sense, implying action in terms described by George Bernard Shaw in another context: 'Thought is a passion.'

In this soliloquy we are present in Hamlet's mind. In Gertrude's speech describing Ophelia's death we have something very different. Whereas Hamlet speaks totally in character, revealing his innermost feelings, the Queen's speech is wholly *out* of character. Her speech is akin to a Chorus in which an event is described for its own sake (as in *Henry V*). It is easy to test this in a crude, oversimple, manner. Had the Queen, as Gertrude, witnessed the event, would she not have attempted Ophelia's rescue? Yet we never ask this question, especially in the theatre. Quite why we don't ask the question is obscure. There is a special justice in the Queen acting as that kind of messenger we associate with Greek tragedy in that it was her incestuous marriage that led to Hamlet's loathing which was transferred to Ophelia – but that hardly explains our failure to note a narrative inconsistency.

Shakespeare possibly forestalls our question by the mythic, storytelling nature of the description. Gertrude does not answer Laertes's 'O, where?' by specifying a particular brook but instead begins with a vague generality of the 'Once upon a time' variety. What follows, as editions with commentaries note, is the kind of floral tribute associated with elegies to the dead; Milton's *Lycidas* has such a 'floral catalogue', for example. We are thus transported from actualities to another, fictional, plane. One of the temptations to which Olivier's film succumbed (because of the ability of film to seem 'more realistic' than the stage) was to show Ophelia drowning. (For this purpose tracks for the camera to run on were laid in a real stream, hidden by weeds, and Ophelia was wafted downstream on an underwater trolley.)

Three minor points might conclude this account of Gertrude's speech. Most productions (including Olivier's film) have Gertrude say 'aslant a brook', following the 1623 text, whereas every edition takes the earlier, less usual, more Shakespearean, form, 'askant the brook'. This is a reasonably legitimate example of simplification in performance for the benefit of a modern audience, a trend evidently apparent soon after Shakespeare's death.

Secondly, there is no direct reference here to Ophelia committing suicide. Line 173 simply says that 'an envious sliver broke'.

Finally, as some editors note (New Arden, p. 544, for example), Shakespeare may have been prompted to the mode of Ophelia's death by an incident that occurred near Stratford when Shakespeare was fifteen. A young woman slipped into the River Avon when going for a pail of water and drowned. Her name was Katherine Hamlett.

5 'RELEVANCE'

'Relevance' is a dangerous word to use when discussing literature, especially drama, but its fashionable over-employment in recent years should not make one too reluctant to mention it. 'Relevance' has been associated with many a production of *Hamlet*, sometimes surprisingly so. The American critic, George Jean Nathan, said of Leslie Howard's *Hamlet* (1936), 'he was the Duke of Windsor out to get Stanley Baldwin and wife, with Winston Churchill playing both Rosencrantz and Guildenstern'. Relevance was not a creation of the 1960s! *Hamlet*'s success stems largely from a very special kind of relevance that has persisted for 400 years. Each age has found something 'relevant' in *Hamlet*. The film historian, Roger Manvell, discussing the Olivier film in 1949, asserted that *Hamlet* 'is a play for our times, since civilisation seems to be passing through a phase of melancholy in the older sense of the word'. What, then, makes it relevant to so many people?

One reason for the play's effectiveness (which is not quite the same as relevance) is a characteristic that has been considered a fault, especially in the eighteenth century: its variety. Garrick in 1772 tried to make it accord to the decorum of his time and, influenced by Voltaire, to remove its 'barbarousness'. As a result, the critic of the *Westminster Magazine* remarked that 'the tedious interruptions of this beautiful tale no longer disgrace it; its absurd digressions are no longer disgusting' (i.e., displeasing).

French adaptations were even more severe. The first *Hamlet* performed in Paris (1769) had no Ghost (though Hamlet addressed him off-stage once), no Gravediggers; Hamlet is King; to maintain decorum, Claudius is not Hamlet's uncle and so does not commit the indecorous sin of incest; and Ophelia is daughter to Claudius. Yet such a travesty of Shakespeare, which held the stage for over eighty years, seemed to Alexandre Dumas in 1818, by when he had neither read the play nor heard of Shakespeare, to be 'a Masterpiece'; it 'made a prodigious impression on me'. It is hard to guess why but Dumas provides a useful clue. Among the things that impressed him were 'the sombre questions put by Doubt to Death'. Such questions have a permanent relevance, and point to that vital tension within the play: Delay (caused by Doubt) and Inevitability (Death). Even in that French version of 1769, this evidently struck home.

Another clue is to be found in two lines which Goethe took to be 'the key to Hamlet's whole procedure':

> The time is out of joint. O, cursèd spite
> That ever I was born to set it right! [I v 188–9]

Shakespeare, wrote Goethe, dramatises 'the effect of a great action laid upon a soul unfit for the performance of it'. Like 'questions put by Doubt to Death', the time is always out of joint for some of us.

The danger for a production that seeks too hard to be relevant is that it might distort. Richard David complained that, though Peter Hall's 1965 RSC production was true to the student anxieties of the time, this was at the expense of 'a Shakespearean dimension'. It is easy for a director to stress his point of view rather than Shakespeare's. A simple way in which this

may be done is by the omission of 'inconvenient' lines. Kozintsev's Soviet film version (1964) omitted, 'And flights of angels
sing thee to thy rest!' [v ii 355], and Claudius, instead of
praying [III iii], soliloquised into a mirror. An even more strik-
ing omission was that from Peter Brook's *King Lear* (1962)
which excluded the sacrifice and solicitude of the servants after
Gloucester's eyes had been put out. Charles Marowitz, who
worked as assistant director on the production, has described
what then happened and, most importantly, the effect
intended:

> Gloucester is covered with a tattered rag and shoved off in the
> direction of Dover. Servants clearing the stage collide with the
> confused blind man and rudely shove him aside. As he is groping
> about pathetically, the house-lights come up – the action continu-
> ing in full light for several seconds afterwards. If this works, it
> should jar the audience into a new kind of adjustment to Gloucester
> and his tragedy.

What *Hamlet* seems always able to offer is that process by which
its hero – we – becomes aware that it is not 'the' fact of life
(which is death) that is so awe-inspiring but, as Robert Orn-
stein put it, the 'anguished discovery of a universe more vast,
more terrible, and more inscrutable than is dreamt of in philo-
sophy'. That must always be relevant. But perhaps it was just
that dimension that led to the Bulgarian government banning
Olivier's film after but a few screenings.

In recent years, however, there have been those who have
reacted against what *Hamlet* may be thought to be saying. Thus
Charles Marowitz wanted his audience to reject, rather than
share, what Hamlet stood for:

> I attempted to delineate a criticism of the type of person Hamlet
> was and, by inference, to indict the values which he represented;
> values which (i.e. misdirected moral concern, intellectual analyses
> as action-substitute etc.) were, in my view, disreputable in our
> society and which derived much of their respectability and
> approval from traditional works such as Shakespeare's *Hamlet*.

This can be seen as a direct development, for a specific non-
Shakespearean purpose, of that manipulation which Marowitz

witnessed in Brook's *King Lear*. Drama – Shakespeare – is here being set, rightly or wrongly, to serve ends other than itself, and in that process, the play as it stands must be undermined. Although that is Marowitz's intention, it is only fair to add that he also explains that his restructuring of a work so widely known 'is an indirect way of making contact with that work's essence', and going over his *Collage Hamlet* I am inclined to agree that it does offer genuine new perspectives on Shakespeare's *Hamlet*.

In what follows it will be seen how *Hamlet* has been 'cut to shape' to fit the needs of conventions and audiences of different periods and how the play's very variety has laid it open to many different interpretations in performance.

PART TWO: PERFORMANCE

6 CUTTING TO SHAPE: THE GLOBE AND THE GARRICK VERSIONS

The First Adaptation

Shakespeare's *Hamlet* (there was definitely an earlier version, possibly by Thomas Kyd, author of the earlier revenge play, *The Spanish Tragedy*, 1590) seems to have been first performed just before or just after the start of the seventeenth century. The short, pirated version of 1603 has differently-named characters (Corambis for Polonius, for example) and is corrupt to the point of being nonsensical in places. This is how 'To be, or not to be' begins (spelling and punctuation modernised):

> To be, or not to be? Aye, there's the point.
> To die, to sleep, is that all? Aye, all.
> No, to sleep, to dream – aye, marry, there it goes.

Said with spurious conviction on the stage it passes muster; but whatever else it is, it is not Shakespeare. A splendid piece of nonsense is found at the equivalent of v i 272, 278: understanding neither 'eisel' (vinegar) nor 'Ossa' (a mountain in Greece), the text combines both to produce 'Make Oosell as a Wart'!

This corrupt version is not wholly without sense. The order of events is at times different, suggesting to some critics a smoother narrative. Gertrude offers to help Hamlet in his stratagem, something that might just possibly be a reminiscence of that earlier, lost, non-Shakespeare *Hamlet*:

QUEEN Hamlet, I vow by that majesty
That knows our thoughts, and looks into our hearts,
I will conceal, consent, and do my best,
What stratagem so'ere thou shalt devise.

This comes immediately prior to the equivalent of Hamlet's lines III iv 214, 216–7. If not to an earlier *Hamlet* it may go back to lines spoken by Belimperia in *The Spanish Tragedy*.

This might lead us to dismiss that version out of hand were it not for a multitude of links with the longer versions and two remarkable characteristics of the 1603 'Bad Quarto', as it is termed. First, on its title-page it states that, in addition to being performed in London, it was also given 'in the two Universities of Cambridge and Oxford, and elsewhere'. Secondly, it betrays evidence of stage business and may thus provide clues to production in Shakespeare's time.

There is no other evidence of the play's being acted at Cambridge and Oxford, and that is a little surprising though not impossible; and the 'elsewhere' sounds rather like advertising puffery. On the other hand the play has a university orientation and some specific university references (see above, p. 10). There is disagreement as to whether *Hamlet* was written with university performance in mind, but that title-page claim is not an inapt pointer for a director, and it may explain the great length and philosophical soliloquising. (The total excision of all these soliloquies from a Polish production of the early 1960s seems the more absurd with this in mind.)

As the play is so long it may well have required cutting for production at the Globe. There is no proof that Shakespeare had a hand in this, though it has a certain commonsense logic about it. The more we associate Shakespeare with the adaptation upon which this corrupt text is based, the more we should have to take account of his authority for some of the stage business – Hamlet's leaping into the grave (see p. 15); the ghost entering the Queen's bedroom 'in his nightgown' [III iv]; Ophelia 'playing on a Lute, and her hair down, singing'; and in the final scene (a detail of the production of Shakespeare's time still often retained), 'They catch one another's Rapiers, and both are wounded'. Further, as a few scholars argue, and the New Penguin edition accepts, the lines thought to be an actor's gag [III ii 43–53] are Shakespeare's, corrupted like much else in this version.

Whether or not Shakespeare had a hand in the version underlying the 1603 text, it represents an adaptation of Shakespeare's own time, just as did the making of the two parts of *Henry IV* into a single play about 1622. In both instances adaptation was resorted to in order to fit the play to the occasion. The theatrical practice of cutting and restructuring is something Shakespeare would have been familiar with. Shakespeare's company had to provide for four kinds of theatre: the Globe (outside); the Blackfriars (indoors); the Court; and on tour. Anyone with experience of presenting plays on tour knows that circumstances dictate adaptation. It would be odd if Shakespeare found that unusual. He might have been surprised (as we can be) to discover *Hamlet* being performed aboard HMS *Dragon* off Sierra Leone in 1607 and 1608, but he would not expect it to be unadapted. We should not, therefore, be surprised or dismayed at adaptation itself. All productions of *Hamlet* are adaptations; Hazlitt was surely right when he said 'There is no play that suffers so much in being transferred to the stage' (1817). Our criteria for assessing adaptations – productions – should take into account the physical dictates of the theatre, the understanding of the audience, and the insight of actors and the director. Adaptations only become travesties when it is not Shakespeare's work that is being realised for an audience but a director's or actor's predilictions. Do we then have adaptation or self-indulgence?

David Garrick's 'Hamlet', 1772

An interesting test of the principles of adaptation can be made by glancing at David Garrick's famous, or infamous, production of 1772. Unlike recent productions, our view of this adaptation is not likely to be stirred by contemporary controversy. What did Garrick do, and why?

David Garrick, as Professors Pedicord and Bergmann (the editors of his *Plays*, the edition referred to here) rightly assert, was '*the* Hamlet for most eighteenth-century playgoers'. He was familiar with Continental theatrical practice; and conversely, his acting of Shakespeare in Paris in 1751, 1763 and 1765 created a sensation. In the eighteenth century it was the norm to make free with the work of earlier dramatists. Thus, Shakespeare's *The Taming of the Shrew* became Garrick's *Catherine and Petruchio* in 1765, the result being described by George Odell in 1920 as 'an excellent farce'.

Garrick first appeared in a version of *Hamlet* acted by Robert Wilks which, though cut, restored some of the omissions made during the Restoration. Garrick twice modified the version he presented (just as Gielgud will be shown to do) in 1751 and 1763. Increasingly Garrick became sensitive to French criticism of the barbarity of *Hamlet* and just before Christmas 1772 he produced his 'Frenchified' version 'to the dismay of many critics and the enthusiasm of London audiences for novelty at any price' as Pedicord and Bergmann put it. We first need to distinguish between Garrick's concern *for* the play as he understood it, and trivialising to please an audience seeking novelty at any price.

Garrick was concerned to cut what he termed 'the rubbish of the fifth act', but he also restored well over 600 lines previously cut from the first four acts. As Pedicord and Bergmann note, although the Dumb Show was left out, the play of 'The Mousetrap' was restored in full. The King at prayer and Hamlet's reaction thereto, and Hamlet's soliloquy, 'How all occasions do inform against me' [IV iv 32–66] were also restored. Certain cuts, such as the Ghost only once calling upon Horatio and Marcellus to swear to keep silent, have commended themselves to later directors – Olivier in his film version, for example. The result, according to Dr G. W. Stone, who discovered the text of the adaptation, was to give 'the eighteenth-century audience a new interpretation of almost all the characters'.

What angered critics then and since was Garrick's treatment of the last act. Eighteenth-century decorum demanded that the Gravediggers go, but there also went much else. Garrick's Act v is made up approximately so (omitting reference to incidental additions and alterations by Garrick):

Garrick V i = Shakespeare IV i, IV ii, and IV iii, the last 11 lines being reduced to 3.
Garrick V ii (which takes place in a wood)
          = Shakespeare IV iv,
                    IV v 1–99
                    v i 250–79
                    40 lines of Garrick's, some based on Shakespeare
Hamlet stabs Laertes (who doesn't die) and kills the King;

The Queen runs out;
Hamlet runs on Laertes's sword;
A Messenger reports that the Queen has fallen into a
     coma;
Just before dying, Hamlet unites the hands of Horatio and
     Laertes;
v ii 354–5 (Now cracks a noble heart . . . thy rest!)
v ii 395–6 (Take up the bodies . . . much amiss).

Now this is no more like Shakespeare than is the Bad Quarto
'To be, or not to be' speech. It is easy to see why the critics were
furious. One of the best critiques was itself a play, Arthur
Murphy's *Hamlet with Alterations* (1772). In this Shakespeare's
Ghost appears to Garrick and says to him:

> I am Shakespeare's Ghost.
> For my foul sins, done in my days of nature
> Doomed for a certain time to leave my works
> Obscure and uncorrected; to endure
> The ignorance of players; the barbarous hand
> Of Gothic editors; the ponderous weight
> Of leaden commentator; fast confined
> In critic fires, till errors, not my own,
> Are done away, and sorely I the while
> Wished I had blotted for myself before.

Though the Ghost is complaining of how his plays have been
murdered, Garrick takes the Ghost's behests to be an invitation
to further adaptation and convinces himself, as well as any
contemporary adapter, of Shakespeare's approval:

> This Ghost is pleased with this my alteration,
> And now he bids me alter all his Plays.
> His plays are out of joint; – *O cursèd spite*:
> That ever I was born to set them right.

Garrick's intentions, the audiences' delight in novelty, and
Murphy's ridicule provide a triangle of forces of a kind that is
still exerted upon Shakespeare's plays. Pedicord and Bergmann neatly contrast 'Garrick's imprudence' with a version of
Hamlet presented by the great American Shakespeare actor,

Maurice Evans, for soldiers during the Second World War. This was called *The G.I. Hamlet* and Evans 'wanted the play to speak with rapid action to the troops'. In this he was so successful that the version later achieved a run of 147 performances on Broadway. Maurice Evans's primary concern was to get Shakespeare across to his soldier audiences, most of whom would not have seen a play by Shakespeare before, not to indulge himself or to use Shakespeare to serve his peculiar interests. The result was no more 'Shakespeare complete' than was Garrick's version, but his approach might help us to distinguish between what is acceptable and what is not in presenting Shakespeare in our day.

7 THE OLIVIER FILM 'HAMLET'

Cinema is not Theatre and film is not drama. The differences are profound and yet, curiously, we may so ignore them and so switch from the one experience to the other, that we can be in danger of assuming similarities that can be deceptive. And television differs from cinema. The prime clue to the difference is to be found in the relationship of the performance to its audience. There are at least four kinds of audience experience. The most familiar and most recent is television. This is usually experienced in a lit room (in the early days rooms were ostentatiously darkened because TV was thought to be like cinema, but we have learned the difference) by a small group of people well-known one to another, often with the distraction of domestic chores or events. At the other extreme, a conventional play is overheard; it is fourth-wall-removed drama; it is attended by a mass of people, possibly many hundreds, who do not know each other and may not, in a cosmopolitan city, even share the same culture. Imagine a performance of a large-scale musical at Drury Lane or an intimate drama such as Pinter's *Old Times* in a smallish theatre, attended by a single couple, one of whom is from time to time reading the newspaper and the other of whom slips out now and again to put the kettle on or let the cat out;

and if the auditorium lights are on, the discomfiture of the performers can be easily imagined. When the lights are left on in an auditorium, the performance, as in a variety show or music hall, may well appeal – speak or sing – directly *to* the audience and not pretend to be overheard. The fourth audience experience is cinema. Like television it has a 'frozen' image, set in a pre-created mould, but, like conventional 'overheard' drama, may be attended by a large, mixed, audience, sitting in the dark.

There are obvious differences between these experiences, but one contrast is particularly worth drawing out. In the previous section (6) it was argued that every theatrical production of a Shakespeare play is an adaptation. It is possible to go further: every performance of every play before a theatre audience is an adaptation of how that production was conceived and rehearsed. The actors make adjustments from the most subtle and unconscious to the deliberate and most marked, depending upon how the audience is responding. How often do actors have to work on an audience to get it to respond as the actors believe they should! Although it is not wholly one-sided, by and large it is the performers who adapt to the audience until they have them 'in their hands'.

Cinema and television work the other way about in that the image is created and set: it is the audience that must adapt, even if, in the home, it does so by choosing this moment rather than that to leave the room. The difference in these audience experiences was brought home to me many years ago when I saw a film version of a Gilbert and Sullivan operetta. In the theatre, these are played with encores. Sometimes an audience will persuade performers to give several encores. In their turn the performers may give each encore, and especially the last, a special twist – topical words, new stage business. Audience and performers are working together to complete the authors' intentions. In the film version an attempt was made to recreate the theatrical tradition of the encore. The audience was invited to applaud songs and the more they applauded the more effect that would have. The result was very hollow. Naturally the producer had a good idea which songs would be most popular and encores were pre-planned and occurred, or didn't occur, irrespective of applause. The effect was comically absurd. A cinema audience could not be made into a theatre audience.

1. The film version of *Hamlet* offers a realism that is not often attempted nowadays in the theatre. Although the influence of the Artistic Director is apparent at this moment in Olivier's film version when, in Act V, sc. i, Hamlet cries out, 'This is I / Hamlet the Dane', the setting is at the opposite extreme to that in the Gielgud/Burton production, in which a table on its side represented a grave and the characters wore contemporary rehearsal dress. Note how the viewer's attention is not directed at any individual. Note also the depth of focus of the scene. The angle permits Laertes's being in the grave to appear wholly natural, which is awkward to portray when a stage-trap is used in a theatre. (Still of the film *Hamlet* by courtesy of The Rank Organisation Plc.)

2, 3. *RSC Production, Stratford, 1965.* The setting for this production arranged for light and darkly oppressive effects. *Above:* the great doors open and the movable faces showing frescoes (Act IV, sc. v). *Below:* the doors closed and the slabs of masonry revealed (Act IV, sc. vi). These illustrations of successive scenes were taken, during a performance, from the lighting box. Photographs: courtesy of the Governors of the Royal Shakespeare Theatre, Stratford-upon-Avon.

4. *RSC Production, Stratford, 1965.* David Warner as Hamlet, with the famous long
    scarf, upbraiding Ophelia (Glenda Jackson). Photograph: courtesy of the Governors
    of the Royal Shakespeare Theatre, Stratford-upon-Avon.

5. *RSC Production, Stratford, 1965.* David Warner as Hamlet. Stage business with the sword at the beginning of Act IV, sc. ii. Photograph © Holte Photographics.

On the credit side, it is probable that a cinema audience is more heterogeneous than is a West End theatre audience, although it may be that the audiences of Shakespeare's day were not quite so all-inclusive as was once believed. For this reason, as well as because until very recently a film's running-time was considerably less than that for a play of the length of *Hamlet*, the text for a film version of a Shakespeare play was subject to considerable cutting and adaptation. A useful comparison might be made with the *The G.I. Hamlet* (mentioned in the previous section (6)). Changes might be made to ensure understanding and avoid misunderstanding. Thus, in Olivier's *Hamlet*, the Queen's solicitude for Hamlet, 'He's fat and scant of breath' [v ii 281], becomes 'He's hot and scant of breath', a change for which there is no authority. ('Fat' means 'sweaty'.)

Advantage can be taken of film's capacity for fluid action to reduce running-time. In Olivier's film, the transition from Ophelia's drowning to the Graveyard scene is effected by the former dissolving into the latter as Gertrude's 'Drowned, drowned' (heard as a voice over the picture) dies away. Skilful use of this capacity for fluidity can also be seen if the moment when Hamlet follows the Ghost [i v] is examined. Olivier is moving round a stairway, his sword-hilt held before him as a protective crucifix. The scene cuts just as he disappears from view and there is a seeming double exposure revealing feet going up steps. These could, in line with the tradition of conventional film cutting, be Olivier's feet but they are those of the Ghost (note the long coat). The audience may experience a momentary uncertainty, slight enough not to jar, sufficient to create increased apprehension.

One of film's outstanding characteristics, its life-likeness, its power to suggest actuality (however deceptive that might be), presents serious temptations for the Shakespeare film-maker. For example, a recent television version of *As You Like It*, and one of the film versions of *A Midsummer Night's Dream*, mistakenly use 'real' locations – a real wood, a real country house. Sometimes this can work. Thus in Olivier's *Henry V* the full-scale cavalry charge, and the realistic battle scenes, do work. This is not so much because what we see is like it really was at the time, as because we are accustomed to such scenes in historical film-dramas and there is a minimum of verse dialogue. In

Hamlet however, this does not work so well. Our suspension of disbelief is shaken when we *see* Ophelia floating downstream, rather like a Millais painting, rather than only hear about it; Gertrude's commentary becomes superfluous. Similarly with the enactment (with rather poor models) of the fight at sea and Hamlet's escape, seen against Horatio's reading of Hamlet's descriptive letter [IV vi]. There is in these instances a confusion of modes, between naturalistic images and imaginative words – words in one instance not even spoken 'in character' (see p. 57).

If this is contrasted to the way the Ghost is presented in the first act, it will be realised that, whether this manifestation is convincing or not, an attempt has been made to harness film's non-realistic capacities in a way that accords with Horatio's first assessment of the apparition: that it is a fantasy [I i 23]. It has also something of that quality of a ghost demanded by Charles Marowitz but so often lacking in theatre productions: the semblance of reality divorced from existence. The accompaniment of heartbeats and what Roger Manvell describes as 'a curious added sound like the singing in one's ears before a fit of fainting', may seem now rather obvious because so often repeated. Although this seems a particularly filmic soundtrack device (to cover footsteps, as it happens), Olivier took it over 'by arrangement' from Jean-Louis Barrault's stage production in Paris, according to Manvell. Olivier was able to use the sound of air and heartbeats to suggest the presence of a no-longer-visible Ghost in III iv. In passing, it is worth noting how difficult it would have been in the film to represent without false laughter the costume used for the Ghost in the early 1600s: a nightgown.

Film enabled one magnificent, strictly cinematic effect to be achieved which effectively involved the audience. When the Ghost leaves at I v 91, the camera is placed on a crane above Hamlet on the battlements. The camera lifts up and away, Hamlet gesturing then fainting below, as if it were the Ghost spirited away and we seem to shift with it. As with all top shots, the film does what the theatre cannot do: shift point of view.

One last distinction between film and theatre requires mention. Film and television (and radio) permit the use of a very intimate kind of voice production. This is not impossible in small theatres but out of the question in such a theatre as Drury

Lane. It is revealing to listen to recordings made 70–80 years ago of Shakespearean actors and to compare them with those by music-hall artists (such as Billy Williams and George Formby Senior) who quickly grasped the intimate nature of the gramophone. The actors are addressing a multitude in a vast theatre; and, of course, that is appropriate for such a speech as 'Once more unto the breach, dear friends'. Olivier developed a camera technique for handling such speeches in *Henry V*. Instead of beginning at a distance and working towards close-up at the climax of the speech (the traditional manner), he reversed that order. That worked well for 'open air' scenes. (But contrast the marvellous intimacy of Henry with the private soldiers on the eve of Agincourt.) It is not surprising in *Hamlet* to find Olivier omitting 'O, what a rogue and peasant slave am I!' apart from three lines when Hamlet says he will 'Play something like the murder of my father' [ii ii 592–4]. Comparison with Richard Burton's delivery of this speech (see section 8, below) will suggest how difficult it would be to give full vent to such a soliloquy on film. Unlike 'To be, or not to be', this is profoundly rhetorical in style. A clue that this is how it has been seen from the very first is to be found in the part-line, 'O, vengeance!' [579]. Harold Jenkins argues that this is an actor's addition. Most editions do include it and most actors make something of it, though the *Spectator* theatre critic, David Benedictus, noted that David Warner spoke the words 'in a tiny, tiny voice'. At the other extreme, Richard Burton can rock the listener with these two words in his recording, divorced though it is from the theatre. This indicates to what extent this is a bravura set-piece for an actor, and it requires amplitude and a theatre audience to make the most of it. There was no place for it in Olivier's film.

Lord Olivier has explained how, 'Quite suddenly, one day, I visualised the final shot of *Hamlet*. And from this glimpse, I saw how the whole conception of the film could be built up.' That last shot showed Hamlet's body being borne up to the height of the castle, set against a stormy sky.* This final vision, Olivier's

---

*The remarkable similarity between this shot and that showing the bringing back of the dead commanding officer after the battle for Goose Green in the recapture of the Falklands suggests how such an image can be unconsciously re-created: such is the power of myth-making.

starting-point, and his initial statement that 'This is the tragedy of a man who could not make up his mind', are the parameters between which Olivier's 'Essay in Hamlet' (as he preferred to call it, rather than 'a film version of a necessarily abridged classic') is set. Notice that Olivier refers to an Essay in Hamlet – not *Hamlet*, the play Manvell described as 'the least immediately filmable of the great poetic tragedies'. Fortinbras, Rosencrantz and Guildenstern are omitted and the film runs an hour less than even the shorter traditional stage versions. Olivier deliberately chose to film in black and white rather than colour, as for *Henry V*, for that made possible deep focus photography (for the first time in England) to which film-makers had become attracted following Orson Welles's *Citizen Kane* (1941). To Desmond Dickinson, in charge of photography, the result was 'not in any revolutionary kind of shot but in the greater illusion of reality it supports'. To Olivier this enabled long sequences to be filmed and made possible beautiful effects. In his account of the film he refers to the scene nicknamed 'The longest distance love-scene on record' [III i]:

> In this scene, Hamlet is sitting in a chair, and through a long series of arches, he sees Ophelia coming towards him. Unknown to Hamlet, she has been warned by her brother, and particularly by her father, to avoid the Prince, and this time, Polonius is hiding behind a pillar. He is invisible to Hamlet, but Ophelia can see him, and when he beckons her away, she turns aside. But to Hamlet, and to the audience who see her from behind Hamlet's shoulders, it looks as though Ophelia has avoided him of her own free will. With the use of deep focus photography, every line of her figure is beautifully distinct as she walks slowly down the long corridors.

Ophelia is again the subject of a long sequence a little prior to her drowning. She is heard singing off-camera and then walks slowly between Horatio and the two sailors (equivalent to IV vi). They leave and the camera follows Ophelia in one lengthy shot as she goes into the next room where are Claudius and Laertes, whose voice can be heard growing louder as Ophelia, and the camera, approach.

One merit we recognise from deep focus filming is the freedom it gives the audience to select what it will view, rather than the director or film editor dictating to the audience by the selection of shots and angles what must be concentrated upon. A useful contrast to 'judging' by the audience is the scene when Claudius is at prayer [III iii 36]. As Hamlet raises his poniard, the camera tilts to reveal more prominently an effigy in the foreground. Olivier is not actually looking at it, but past it, as he speaks; but the presence of this sacred image is brought prominently to the attention of the film audience. This camera movement is akin to stage business. What must be questioned is whether such business is appropriate here. The impression is given that the effigy causes Hamlet to relent; in fact, Hamlet refrains from killing Claudius because he believes [85] falsely [97–8] that Claudius has purged his soul and he will but despatch 'this same villain / To heaven' [77–8]. Notice also how, in filming the play-within-the-play [III ii], the camera tracks behind the King so that we see from his point of view and, from his hand movement gripping the throne, realise his perturbation.

An obvious manipulation of our response is Olivier's displacement of 'To be, or not to be' [III i 56–89] from before the consignment of Ophelia to a nunnery [III i 140] to later in the film, the transition being made by non-realistic camerawork, rising away from Ophelia upwards to the top of the battlements. Roger Manvell succinctly juxtaposed the cinematic and interpretive considerations of this change in a broadcast:

> Although we may question the wisdom of this transposition, since it gives an entirely new and commonplace reason for his desire to commit suicide (namely the betrayal of his love by Ophelia), it makes an effective visual climax, since this section of the film works its way up to the topmost pinnacle of the castle for the soliloquy.

As he pointed out earlier, 'film is the art of observing action, . . . In the cinema it is always the eye that has the advantage of the ear. Words too easily lose their hold on the attention while the eye concentrates on the actor and the scene.' One other device Olivier used to solve the problem of soliloquies (besides omission and transposition) was by playing voice over picture, a device that had been used some years earlier for the internal thoughts of characters in O'Neill's *Strange Interlude*.

The use of black and white film enabled Olivier to make good use of darkness and light. Ophelia's chamber has a lightness and freshness that, while being appropriate, creates its effect cinematically. Less expected is the light, open-air character of 'To be, or not to be', with its counterpoint of battlements and the sea crashing below (= perturbation of spirit?). It now looks stereotyped, but the conjunction of dark thoughts and daylight setting is still effective.

The lighter tone is wholly appropriately hit off in the exchanges between Hamlet and the First Gravedigger (played by Stanley Holloway, a music-hall star who later achieved fame in *My Fair Lady*). The light smile that plays round Olivier's face, subtly revealed by the close-up camerawork, illuminates how he has come to terms with mortality.

Two further aspects of the film are worth mentioning. Twice Olivier uses silent-film technique. Both show the killing of Hamlet's father: the first time vignetted to illustrate the Ghost's account, and the second time for the Dumb Show that precedes the spoken play-within-play. The first of these is a distracting elaboration; the second succeeds brilliantly. It was a stroke of genius of 'an inspired and imaginative amateur' film-producer (as Manvell calls Olivier) to use an out-dated film technique for what, even in Shakespeare's day, was an antique device.

Secondly, the music. In Shakespeare's plays there is much music. *King Lear* has over twenty songs: John Marston's *The Dutch Courtesan* (1605) provides actors with lines calling for music between each act. In its provision of music, Olivier's film *Hamlet* is closer to Elizabethan practice than many a stage production – though it should be noted that the RSC makes frequent use of live music in its productions.

One last virtue of film and television, and of this production in particular. Stage productions are ephemeral. What was seen last night, last week, a decade ago, cannot now be recalled accurately. Film, especially transferred to video as *Hamlet* has been, can be seen again and again. That means that what is said here can be checked and there is evidence for disagreement.

8   GIELGUD AND BURTON: 1934 AND 1964

Shakespeare was born in 1564 and the 400th anniversary of his birth saw celebrations throughout the world. In Toronto and New York Sir John Gielgud directed Richard Burton as Hamlet. Ten days after the New York opening the production was recorded; and later a regular performance before an audience at the Lunt-Fontaine Theater on Broadway was filmed. The quality of the acting was very uneven, at times being quite bad, and the whole production was at too strident a pitch. Only Eileen Herlie – who had played the Queen in the Olivier film – and George Rose, the First Gravedigger, seemed to avoid being infected by the intensity of Burton's approach.

Recordings are too often spoken of as 'dynamic' but that word can truly be applied to Burton's performance, especially the 'Rogue and peasant slave' speech, to which attention will be directed here. Gielgud's direction of Burton is particularly interesting. He was himself a famous Hamlet and his performance in London in 1934–5 and in New York in 1936–7 was described in detail by Rosamond Gilder long before theatrical 'log-books' became fashionable. Further, Gielgud himself added an essay, 'The Hamlet Tradition', which, like the account of the production, is invaluable. The 1964 production has been written up, partly from tape-recordings, by Richard L. Sterne. He had permission to take notes but introduced the tape-recorder secretly, once hiding for six hours under the stage so that he could record a private rehearsal, held by Gielgud and Burton, behind closed and guarded doors. This he thought the most valuable part of his record for in this rehearsal Gielgud stated what he thought the play meant:

> I don't agree with Larry [Olivier], who said in the film that this is a play about a man who can't make up his mind. Surely it's about a man who cannot reconcile his own conscience with the world as he sees it, but who is able to come to this reconciliation by the end of the play.

To Gielgud, the journey to England solves all:

> he comes back fantastically ready to carry out his mission without

complications. It's only the sight of Ophelia's body and Laertes jumping into the grave, in which Hamlet suddenly sees this young man whom he always had liked behaving exactly as *he* had done when *his* father died, in a sort of hysteria of grief. That makes him jump in and do all that violent stuff.

(See above, pp. 15–16.)

From his contribution to Rosamund Gilder's book, and her and Sterne's accounts (to all of which I am indebted), it is possible to see Gielgud's sensitive awareness of the tradition he inherited and the delicate way he refrained from imposing his conception on Burton.

> Gielgud discussed with Burton the possibilities for Hamlet's death. In his own performance Gielgud fell into Horatio's arms. He suggested using the Forbes-Robertson staging of dying, in which Hamlet sits on the throne, with the possible variation of getting up at the last minute and finally falling to the ground.

Gielgud's subtlety of performance was ever attempting to modify the vigour of Burton's approach. Thus at III ii 353–79, Burton set out to teach Guildenstern to play the recorder 'with a lot of shouting' whereas 'Gielgud wanted the scene ironic and bitter, yet mocking'. Their combined work is to be heard at its most effective in Burton's recording of the 'Rogue and peasant slave' soliloquy.

Rosamond Gilder's description of Gielgud's 1934 interpretation of this speech shows points of similarity with and difference from Burton's approach. At line 559 she describes how Gielgud

> swings round, facing front, his clenched fist thrust down, his head back, his voice rising in a tornado to the crest of '*amaze indeed* the very faculties of eyes and ears'. Then, suddenly, a drop – voice, body, carriage all deflated. He moves slowly to the stool at the left hand of the table and falls on it, vanquished.

Burton's attack from 'What's Hecuba to him' to '. . . faculties of eyes and ears' [556–67] owes something to the Welsh tradition of *hwyl*, that characteristic step by step raising of the level of intensity so expressive of the fervour of Welsh preaching of an earlier generation. Burton starts almost conversationally and raises the pitch in six stages on 'What would he do', 'He would drown', 'Make mad', 'Confound', 'and amaze'. But at 'Yet I', his voice becomes almost falsetto, a brilliant equivalent of Gielgud's deflation.

Unlike Gielgud, whose 'Am I a coward?' [568] was a 'bitter self-challenge' followed by a 'swift, staccato exclamation', Burton is almost quizzical on 'Am I a coward?' but rapidly generates a crescendo of fury; his staccato effect is reserved for the very last syllable of the speech, coming after a distinct pause in the line;

> Wherein I'll catch the conscience # # of the King.

The last three words are run almost into one. The climax of Burton's lines 568–73 is cut short most dramatically on a half-strangled cry of 'Ha'.

Almost inevitably, if 'O vengeance' is accepted (see p. 51), it forms a great climax of the section from 'Ha' at line 573. Gielgud thought Burton's treatment of 'Ha' was 'too showy'. He wanted something simple (but didn't seem to get it in either recording or filmed performance – an indication of an unresolved tension between the approaches of the two men). Gielgud advised:

> save your climax for the 'O vengeance'. Can you give the impression of stabbing him on that line? Try the same gesture you use in the prayer scene of the sword over your head. Then try sinking on the arm of the chair, exhausted, for 'Why, what an ass am I'. (Burton does this.) That's good. Now stay sitting for 'about my brain!' You've already thought of it once before the scene. Suddenly, at last, you're back to your first thesis. That's why the whole speech must be slow.

Rosamond Gilder describes Gielgud's own performance so:

> he leans against the table – half sitting – his agitation slowly mounting, this time to a final climax of horror as the hated uncle is excoriated in hissing, virulent words – 'treacherous, *lecherous, kindless* villain!' Hamlet is trembling with fury, his body shaking, his voice high. With 'Vengeance!' he snatches his dagger from its sheath and rushes to the doorway, right, throwing himself against it

as the wave of his futile fury crashes to its height and dies. His raised arm falls, the dagger rolls on the ground, his body sways against the door and he sinks, almost crouching, on the top step.

The downward sweep of his self-scorn is as devastating as the upward sweep of his rage. His voice is broken with a sob of humiliation.

Burton follows much this pattern, but achieves what can only be called a *coup de théâtre*. I know of nothing like it. Richard Sterne describes the genesis of Burton's 'O vengeance'.

> Gielgud suggested that Burton alter his reading of 'O vengeance!' Burton had been reading it with a long wail on the final syllable of the word: 'O *ven*geance!' (Note: Burton first hit upon the idea for his celebrated reading of the line – a long, sustained, descending glissando on '*O*' followed by tearful and almost inaudible 'vengeance' – during his opening-night performance in New York.)

In the filmed stage-performance, 'O vengeance' is quite different; it is much shorter, and the 'O' is punctuated and cut short by a kind of 'Ha-Ha' sound.

No description can do justice to the stunning effect Burton achieved. It demanded not only technique and imagination, but courage. Burton was bringing into the late twentieth century a vocal resource more associated with melodramatic claptrap. The risk was enormous, but, in my view, thrillingly dramatic, at least in the speech heard in isolation: it is indeed a cadenza – a word used by Gielgud to describe the soliloquies in his note on the recording. And inevitably he took the chance of laying himself open to the critic eager to point to Hamlet's advice:

> in the very torrent, tempest, and, as I may say, whirlwind of your passion, you must acquire and beget a temperance that may give it smoothness. O, it offends me to the soul to hear a robustious periwig-pated fellow tear a passion to tatters, to very rags, to split the ears of the groundlings.
>
> [III ii 5–10]

Burton came close to falling into the trap which, Gielgud maintains, lies in wait for all playing Hamlet: 'The scenes themselves are so strikingly dramatic that they may betray the actor into sheer effectiveness (in the theatrical sense).' The contrast with the gentlemanly, controlled Forbes-Robertson recording of the early 1920s is quite extraordinary. Forbes-Robertson lets his brief 'O' trail away; his 'vengeance' recovers a little, but the whole expression is almost an afterthought rather than a climax. It is then followed by a series of pent-up sobs. Like other actors of his generation, he pronounces 'my', as in 'unpregnant of my cause' as 'me'.

Whereas Gielgud is very sensitive to theatrical tradition and discriminates finely between what is valuable and what is dross (see below, regarding stage business), Burton, possibly inherently, has an astonishing power to put to use in an acceptable twentieth-century manner those nineteenth-century vocal techniques for which the teachers of that time strove. It must, though, be admitted that when every speech but 'Now all occasions do inform against me' is delivered at high pitch, it makes excessive demands on an audience – especially as in this production such intensity was catching and was imitated by almost every actor.

In 1906, Grenville Kleiser had his *How to Speak in Public* published in New York. He drew on his experience as an instructor in public speaking at Yale University and so wrote with authority. He described (and provided exercises for attaining) five 'modulations' of voice: quality, pitch, time, inflection, and force. Quality was subdivided into seven kinds: Simple Pure (conversational), Orotund (unusual fulness), Aspirated, Oral (the quality of weakness), Falsetto, Guttural, and Pectoral (a 'deep hollow chest-tone'), to which he added the Whisper. Each had special functions. Thus: Guttural for revenge, anger or horror; Pectoral for awe, remorse and deep terror. And the quality had to be matched to the words to be uttered. Every one of these eight characteristics is to be found used, dramatically effectively and beautifully integrated, in Burton's 'O, what a rogue' speech. It is most unlikely that Burton was consciously adapting these qualities; they arose from his natural gifts, his flair, and Gielgud's direction. It is possible elsewhere from Sterne's rehearsal record to see Gielgud calling on Burton's qualities of voice. For the 'fall of a sparrow' speech [v ii 214–6], Gielgud asked Burton to give three distinct colors to the line. 'If it be now, 'tis not to come' (outward quality); 'If it be not to come, it will be now' (introspective); 'if it be not now, yet it will come' (warmly to Horatio).

One or two further examples might be illuminating. Thus, the name in 'For Hecuba' is split into three separately accentuated syllables and given a guttural touch, but the most pronounced guttural effect is reserved for lines 577–8 ('Bloody . . . kindless villain!'). In 'And can say nothing, no, not for a king' [566], the voice is aspirated on 'nothing', becoming pectoral for the rest of the line. But the most dangerous use of a nineteenth-century technique (after 'O, vengeance!') is the sudden descent to the pectoral for 'the murder' in 'Play something like the murder of my father' [593]; and again, it works brilliantly. Throughout the play Burton would descend into the pectoral for a single word or phrase. Michael Pennington, in the RSC 1980 *Hamlet*, used the pectoral voice much less convincingly, when refraining from killing Claudius, for the line ' 'A took my father grossly, full of bread' [III iii 80].

In 1934 Gielgud spoke 'I'll have grounds / More relative than this' [601–2] as 'a cry of despair and defiance', with the final line-and-a-half

> spoken in a frenzy of excitement, reaching this time in one burst the summit of intensity. His body is galvanized: he hurls himself across the intervening space to the chair at the end of the table where he has sat listening to the Player. He pulls the paper towards him, seizes a pen; the light catches his wildly excited face, then blacks out as he bends forward writing frantically.

Thirty years later, Burton was to give a totally different interpretation. 'I'll have grounds' was light, almost teasing; the final line-and-a-half was whispered, as if he were naughtily and secretly letting the audience in on a secret.

Gielgud's business of writing madly on his tablets (the lines to be inserted into *The Mousetrap* presumably) was derived from a nineteenth-century production by Sir Henry Irving. Gielgud *knew* this was false and that he should, as Shakespeare indicates, exit. But he wrote that he never believed he could succeed as Hamlet until the applause came at that moment in the play on first nights; he had to play for applause here for his self-confidence. The fall of the curtain (then customary, now unusual) as Hamlet was seen to be starting his plot in motion prompted that applause. He goes on:

> At later performances, however, I have been, and still am, irritated by my actor's desire to make such a 'curtain' of it. If we could bury the play for twenty years we might perhaps feel it mattered less how certain parts of it would be received than whether the great speeches would be correctly interpreted in their own place in the play.

One of the most difficult aspects of a play to recover in reading is stage business: those actions, often tiny, sometimes exaggerated, that communicate meaning in a non-verbal manner. Thus, Claudius's tension when watching the Dumb Show in Olivier's film is revealed by his 'business' of gripping the arm of his throne. He has nothing to say but this little gesture conveys how he is responding. In *King Lear*, Lear's knights are accused of behaving badly. Shakespeare, as too often, gives no indication as to how they behave – he would have been on the spot to say what he wanted. If they are rowdy, that supports the complaint; if they are well-behaved, then the complaint is malicious. How the play is understood depends here on how the director instructs the knights to behave. When the ballet dancer, Robert Helpmann, turned actor and played Hamlet in London in February 1944 (he was later to play the Bishop of Ely in Olivier's film of *Henry V*), a critic, George Barker, commented adversely on his stage business:

> His dramatic Hamlet seemed to me a little too choreographic. Thus, I do not consider it histrionically proper that Hamlet should indicate a climax of his emotion by tapping his foot on a bottom step. I also do not consider it histrionically proper that his first encounter with the ghost of the elder Hamlet should leave the younger Hamlet worming his way round the stage on his stomach. For, whereas such gymnastics could, in terms of the dance, express an excess of emotion, they succeed in expressing, in terms of the dramatic, little more than a misconception of how human beings behave.

Hamlet is himself concerned with this topic (and we must not confuse Hamlet with Shakespeare): 'do not saw the air too much with your hand, thus . . . Suit the action to the word, the word to the action' [III ii 4–5, 17–18]. Grenville Kleiser, 300 years later, naturally paid attention to this: 'Don't make too many gestures with the same hand. . . . Too few gestures are better than too many. . . . When possible, one gesture should glide into the next.' He goes on to describe appropriate gestures, suiting them to words, the gesture being given precisely on the first italicised word:

One hand supine – middle zone: 'What trade are *thou?*'
One hand supine – ascending: 'Fix your eyes upon *excellence*'
One hand prone – descending: 'To thy *knees* and beg for pardon'
Both hands vertical – ascending: '*O horror, horror, horror*'; or, rather contradictorily, perhaps: '*Victory! Victory! Victory!* is the shout!'

It is easy to smile at this: it reads like the gestures given to cartoon characters on TV; though in a carefully stylised form, as used by the visiting actors in the Gielgud/Burton production, the effect is appropriate and convincing. Gielgud is thinking of something more subtle, but the weight of the power of tradition in matters of stage business is plain from his reaction to it. Having said how much he deplores 'stage business and the Victorian and Edwardian traditions of Shakespeare', he goes on:

At the same time I know only too well that my own performance has been cluttered with these things. I have never been either sufficiently experienced or sufficiently original to dare to direct or play *Hamlet* without including a great deal of this kind of theatricalism, for fear of being unable to hold the interest of the audience by a more classical and simple statement of the written text. As in music, it needs the greatest artists to perform most simply and perfectly the greatest composition.

That, of course, was Gielgud half-a-century ago and now the 'simple statement' has been perfected.

The effect of unreasoning stage business ('Do not saw the air too much . . .', 'Don't make too many gestures . . .') is well illustrated by Gielgud's attempt to place that purple-passage speech, 'To be, or not to be' more firmly in character, rather than taking it as a set piece for which the audience has been waiting all evening. 'The quality of mercy' speech in *The Merchant of Venice* presents very similar problems.

> I imagined I created a great innovation by walking about in this speech and was extremely proud of the way I slipped in the opening words, trying to make not too long a pause before them, and to get under way before the audience was quite sure it really was the big speech. But, of course, this defeated its own ends in time. When I did the play in New York I became self-conscious in the walking, and after a few nights Mrs Patrick Campbell, who came to see the play, implored me to cut it out, as she said that watching the movements distracted from the words and destroyed the essential sense of composure necessary for the full effect of the lines.

In his direction of Burton's *Hamlet*, Gielgud would eliminate business introduced during the course of rehearsal, such as the two servants who ran across the stage with Laertes's trunk at 'Your servants tend' [I iii 83], because he thought it distracting, and of having Ophelia sew during this scene, because he thought it was 'lost' on stage. Sometimes business can be influenced by extra-theatrical considerations. Gielgud recalled a piece of business that Alec Guinness had used:

> *Gielgud* When he said to Ophelia in the play scene, 'That's a fair thought to lie between a maid's legs', he reached right up her skirts in front of the whole court.
> *Burton* Well, John, that's good for Alec, but I'm liable to get a sexy reputation.
> *Gielgud* I could add a program note.

Sometimes an almost false comedy might be invented. At IV iii 51 Hamlet says to the King, just as he is despatched for England, 'Farewell, dear mother'. On being reminded that Claudius is his 'loving father', Hamlet sardonically replies that man and wife are one flesh. Gielgud had Burton 'run up and kiss the King on the cheek just before saying "Farewell, dear mother" ', and this, as Sterne reports, became one of Burton's favourite bits of business. On occasion, Burton would take as great risks with business as with his voice. Thus, in the 'Rogue and peasant slave' speech, at 'Who calls me villain?', he whirled about 360°, not once but twice.

Other business proposed – such as the stabbing of the throne at 'O, vengeance!' with a prop-sword left behind by the Players, though first proposed by Gielgud (compare Gielgud's own business in 1934, mentioned above) – was later considered by him an awful cliché and not appropriate to the style of this production. An interesting sidelight on the element of improvisation in Burton's work, even when so carefully prepared, was his reaction: 'I wouldn't like to rely on a prop, John, *in case I change my mind in performance*' (my italics).

Yet it is not ultimately the incidentals of stage business that give distinction and individuality to a performance. What gives business life is the quality of the actor, and this is well illustrated by Rosamond Gilder's description of Gielgud in the 1934 production watching the Players perform before Claudius:

> His right hand holds the two pages of manuscript in a grip so tight the edges curl. In his crouching immobility he seems to radiate force. He drives the players on with his pulsing excitement.

There is no movement here, only a position. Though Gielgud did beat the rhythm of the lines spoken by the Players once or twice, the intense power of the moment comes from within the actor. Business, like the voice, must be the extension of that power, not an embellishment for its own sake.

In discussing the Gielgud–Burton *Hamlets* most stress has been placed on the speaking of lines, stage business and dramatic tradition. For Peter Hall's *Hamlet* attention will be particularly given to set and costume; and finally, for the Charles Marowitz *Collage Hamlet*, the way a play's meaning and significance can be challenged will be discussed.

9 THE ROYAL SHAKESPEARE COMPANY'S 'HAMLET', 1965

The programme for the Royal Shakespeare Company's *Hamlet* in 1965 carried a number of extracts from writers and critics designed to illuminate the play. One of these was particularly valuable. It was by William Blake: 'He who desires but acts not, breeds pestilence.' It may be that one of Hamlet's problems is that, fundamentally, he does not wish to take revenge; but applied to *Hamlet* it suggests, intriguingly, that Hamlet is, as much as Denmark itself, a source of corruption.

Peter Hall, in a short essay outlining how he saw the play, offers a profoundly pessimistic view of the society for which he presented his *Hamlet*.

> For our decade I think the play will be about disillusionment which produces an apathy of the will so deep that commitment to politics, to religion or to life is impossible. . . . There is a sense of what-the-hell anyway, over us looms the Mushroom Cloud. And politics are a game and a lie, whether in our country or in the East/West dialogue which goes on interminably without anything very real being said. This negative response is deep and appalling.

The outcome, in *Hamlet* and in society, seems for Hall to be dictatorship:

> I don't find *Hamlet* a tragedy in the sense that at the end of it I am left ennobled, purged, and regenerated. I think it belongs with *Troilus and Cressida* and *Measure for Measure* as a clinical dissection of life. It is a shattering play, a worrying play; and at the end you are left with Fortinbras, the perfect military ruler. And I don't know about you, but I would not particularly like to live in Denmark under Fortinbras.

I am reminded of a student production which, though in a generally 'Elizabethan' costume, concluded with Fortinbras entering at the end of the play in khaki uniform with a Nazi swastika armlet. It was a gimmick, of course, but a vivid and telling point. Incidentally, the grouping of *Hamlet* with two Problem Plays was first suggested at the end of the nineteenth century by F. S. Boas.

The apathy of will which Hall saw in the play he transferred to the new generation then growing to maturity, especially in universities. Hamlet, Hall said, saw through Claudius ('a superb operator who hardly ever lost his nerve' – at least, not in Hall's production, for he treated Hamlet's attempt to expose him through *The Mousetrap* with the disdain due one who had committed a social gaffe); and he saw through Polonius, who, to Hall was 'not a doddering old fool but the kind of shrewd, tough, establishment figure you can still meet in St James's'. In the 1980 RSC production he was to remain a 'nosing, dangerous politician, not yet superannuated' according to Gareth Lloyd Evans. Charles Marowitz's views of Claudius and Polonius are not dissimilar from Hall's. He goes on to suggest that Hamlet is a poor judge of character because Polonius plays the fool when with him, though at other times (even when Polonius is talking with his children presumably) there is nothing of the 'foolish prating knave' about him, and from all we see, 'Claudius is an efficient monarch and a tactful politician' – a view that goes back to Wilson Knight in 1930:

> Claudius, as he appears in the play, is not a criminal. He is – strange as it may seem – a good and gentle king, enmeshed by the chain of causality linking him with his crime. . . . The question of the relative morality of Hamlet and Claudius reflects the ultimate problem of this play.

Hall's Hamlet was a long-scarved student of a kind increasingly familiar in the late 1960s. (See Plate 4.) Warner's scarf did get shorter as the run went on (and seemed to have been inherited by Horatio in the 1980 RSC production). Scarves must have been a theatrical fashion in 1964. The modern-dress First Player had one in the Gielgud/Burton *Hamlet* and for a while it was borrowed by Hamlet.

Hall's point of departure in directing his very young Hamlet (David Warner was only 24) stemmed from his attitude to politics and The Establishment. He saw Claudius and Polonius as politicians and who must, therefore, lie and cheat:

> And Hamlet refuses this. The young must feel this about their rulers even when there is no crime in question. They must believe

that the millenium could come tomorrow if power were in the right hands.

The critics did not wholly approve. *The Times* protested: 'Polonius *is* a silly old man. Osric *is* a fop. Claudius *does* suffer from remorse and can be publicly unnerved.' That critic described Claudius's calling for lights at the end of the play-within-the-play as if he were merely rebuking Hamlet for a social gaffe, in marked contrast to tradition (as in, say, the Olivier film). David Warner, said Penelope Gilliatt in the *Observer*, was much more like a redbrick undergraduate than a wronged heir apparent. (The several references to this Hamlet being a 'redbrick' undergraduate make one wonder whether he might have been acceptable to the critics had he been obviously Oxbridge.) Warner, said David Benedictus, bit his nails, scratched his face during a soliloquy, and wiped his brow from time to time. Furthermore, this *Hamlet* was a test of endurance. Though over 700 lines were cut, the remaining 3,100 took, according to the programme, $2\frac{1}{2}$ hours for Part One and 1 hour and 10 minutes for Part Two. The running time became rather less as time went by, and a short five-minute break was introduced after I v when the production returned to Stratford in 1966.

Now, all those derogatory comments are soundly based. In theory I can agree with each and every point. Yet, though my generation was that which David Warner's Hamlet was supposedly inveighing against, that $2\frac{1}{2}$-hour Part One held me enthralled and the whole production is etched sharply on my memory as no other is. That impression counts for nothing. It is mentioned because a critic, however good, sees but a part of a play, on a particular occasion, and out of one kind of experience. Peter Hall *did* manipulate Shakespeare's *Hamlet*; he was, perhaps, too concerned with social relevance; but he hit upon, *in Shakespeare*, something that was beginning to work its way through our academic system until, in Paris, at Berkeley, even near-by at politically apathetic Birmingham, it burst forth. There is a way in which the adverse comment that Hall's Student Prince attracted was to the point, yet Hall sensed something in the air and imaginatively gave it expression through Shakespeare. This was very different from the self-

indulgence of which theatre directors and actors may sometimes stand accused.

For the Gielgud–Burton *Hamlet* the cast wore rehearsal
clothes. Richard Sterne describes how one particular garment
evolved:

> Burton appeared at the afternoon rehearsal wearing a black v-neck
> sweater. Gielgud liked it and told him to wear it for the perfor-
> mance. A tailor took Burton's measurements and made five dupli-
> cates of the sweater.

Gielgud decided that the play would be acted 'as if it were the
final run-through before the technical rehearsals begin, and
play it in rehearsal clothes, stripped of all extraneous trap-
pings'. This could have an incongruous effect. When Polonius
said that the apparel oft proclaims the man, he had some
business with his raincoat. At his 'not gaudy', this got a laugh –
but a laugh that was, I guess, the product of an inapt distraction. He did intend to include 'a few beautiful period props'
which he thought would seem the more interesting for being
seen against the actors' ordinary clothes – though what was
selected seemed as plain as the clothes. Obviously there had to
be *some* sort of set and it had to be lit at least sufficiently for the
audience to be able to discern what was going on. Gielgud
explained:

> Ben Edwards has designed a set which looks like the walls of an
> empty theatre, with high, double-dock doors in the center at the
> back, and ropes and weights hanging from the grid. Some plain,
> rough rostrums will be arranged in front of the back wall, giving
> various levels and steps and ramps leading to exits left and right.
> The lighting must seem to be ordinary rehearsal lighting. . . . But
> . . . there'll be no sudden blackouts, no sudden changes of light to
> startle [the audience's] concentration.

This reads better than it looked. There was a soot-and-
whitewash effect which was aggravated by the use of a following spot from time to time. Charles Marowitz was even more
outspoken about scenery:

> I loathe theatre scenery because it is like a phonograph-record
> caught in a groove; it repeats itself endlessly while the play pro-

gresses. No scenery I have ever seen can keep up with the progress of a play like *Hamlet* because it really takes place in the actor's and spectator's shifting consciousness. . . . The recesses of Hamlet's mind are our flies.

Olivier's film sets had about them, almost inevitably because the medium was film, a touch of realism. We seem to be in a real castle in Elsinore, with real battlements, with a real sea crashing around, and real stairs, of which dramatic – filmic – use is made. Nevertheless, the designer, Roger Furse, was concerned more with psychological than physical reality. In explaining this he gave away a fascinating secret about the seemingly massive pillars in the Council Chamber:

> Art departments these days can imitate anything and can produce real-life sets; but this seems to me missing an opportunity to create atmosphere. Distortions of actual scenery will not be resented mentally by an audience, but they will be sensed psychologically and will add to the dramatic effect of the film. Thus, in the Council Chamber scenes of *Hamlet*, we have put our massive pillars on wheels and, for certain shots, have moved the pillars up and down the room.

John Bury's sets for the 1965 RSC production fell between these extremes. As is more usual nowadays, there is no proscenium curtain at Stratford (compare Gielgud's use of the curtain, section 8 above) just as there was none at the Globe. However, for this production a broad, heavy, black proscenium was built with the fore-part of the stage thrust out from it. The floor was unevenly patterned in black-and-white squares with, as the need arose, a brightly-lit triangular area, or a central circular spot. The angled rear walls had between them two huge studded doors into one of which was set a small wicket gate. In each of the rear walls were two openings, some three times higher than they were wide and into each were fitted prism-shaped structures (like the *periáktoi* of the Ancient Greek theatre). These could be turned to show the different faces which represented stone slabs, memorial tablets, bookcases (for a study), geometric designs, or tapestry-like representations of naked classical figures to suggest luxurious living.

The sense of place could thus be rapidly changed, conveying mood without being divorced from realism. To show the graveyard, the double doors were opened, a fractured stone memorial was visible and the faces of the wall-structures showed the memorial tablets. (Two aspects of this set are shown in Plates 2 and 3.)

As in Olivier's film, much use was made of a large cannon, suggesting preparations for war [I i 71–8], or for idle discharge at festivities [I iv 6*sd* and v ii 262–4]. For the Council Meeting of I ii, a diamond-shaped table, with Claudius, Gertrude, Polonius and Hamlet already sitting at it, was rolled in as a single unit. This, according to Robert Speaight, showed Hamlet trapped in a 'cage of circumstances', but to Stanley Wells looked a trifle ludicrous. Inevitably what seem good ideas have a habit of working out differently in practice.

It is usual, especially in England, for those of the theatre to despise academics. Thus Gielgud during the Toronto run of his *Hamlet*:

> Some lunatic rang me up from the University yesterday with a lot of idiotic ideas. He said the songs in the mad scene should be 'hot-cha-cha'. But that got me to thinking . . .

Thinking! The 1980 RSC *Hamlet* was in part attributed to the Introduction that Anne Barton (wife of the play's director) had written for the late Professor T. J. B. Spencer's New Penguin edition of the play. This discussed the significance of the theatrical allusions in the play, something analysed by Maynard Mack in 1952:

> The most pervasive of Shakespeare's image patterns in this play, however, is the pattern evolved round the three words, 'show', 'act', 'play'. 'Show' seems to be Shakespeare's unifying image in *Hamlet*. Through it he pulls together and exhibits in a single focus much of the diverse material in this play. . . . 'Act' . . . I take to be the play's radical metaphor. It distills the various perplexities about the character of reality into a residual perplexity about the character of an act. What, this play asks again and again, is an act? What is the relation to the inner act, the intent? . . . the third term, 'play' . . . is a more precise word, in Elizabethan parlance at least, for all the elements in *Hamlet* that pertain to the art of the theater

... we see that every major personage in the tragedy is a player in some sense, and every major episode a play.

The effect was *of the theatre* without being fully theatrical, as Tom Matheson wrote:

> We are in the theatre and not allowed to forget it . . . a forestage occupied by a bare, raised, wooden platform; in the gloomy recesses behind it stands a half-revealed assembly of heavily shrouded properties: a huge, wicker, costume-basket; a tarnished wooden throne; a clutch of foils and pikes . . . These emblems of theatrical illusion are visible throughout the performance. We are not to be transported to Elsinore, to the court and the graveyard; we remain instead in the world of impersonation. . . . Paradoxically, conventional theatricality is almost entirely missing from this disciplined and rational re-creation.

The costumes for Olivier's film version were elaborate in the tradition of historical film drama. Peter Hall's production came between that and Gielgud's rehearsal clothes. Hamlet had his red scarf and Claudius and Polonius added to their quasi-Elizabethan costumes the pin-stripe waistcoats associated with the twentieth-century Establishment. One unintended effect of this was to suggest that, despite all, the Establishment survived. Fortinbras appeared at the end of the play as a kind of Knight in Shining Armour (Silver according to *The Stage*). That irony might be taken at face value by an audience.

One or two tiny points. Elizabeth Spriggs as the Queen vomited so violently and realistically at the end of the play that mimesis and reality were in danger of coming into conflict (not to mention those of the audience nearby). The rolling-on of the oversize Ghost on his trolley was effective in the night scenes in the first act but incongruous when he loomed up behind the arras stretched across the opened double doors in the Queen's bedroom in III iv. Much more effective was a little additional business at the beginning of IV ii when Hamlet thrust the sword with which he had just killed Polonius into a gap between the paving slabs and knelt before it, seemingly in prayer, the hilt once again forming a crucifix. (See Plate 5.) Each of these three incidents is indicative of the razor-edge which distinguishes effectiveness from failure in the creation of stage business.

72

10 Marowitz's 'Collage Hamlet'

In Penelope Gilliatt's words, Peter Hall's 1965 *Hamlet* was 'specifically social'; it had, said Alan Brien, the atmosphere of a teach-in. Rightly or wrongly, well or badly, it was speaking directly about issues of the time refracted through Shakespeare. However, the twentieth-century pin-stripe waistcoat worn by two sixteenth-century politicians suggested a greater degree of permanence for the Establishment than Hall intended. Charles Marowitz was concerned in his *Hamlet* to *challenge* society's assumptions rather than offer a critique. And it was time, he argued, for this classic to be declassicised. The play, like much of Shakespeare's drama, is, according to Marowitz, a 'reworking and rehashing [of] the commonplace narratives of his day' and our conception of Hamlet 'is composed of first- and second-hand memories of actors' from Booth to Olivier. As a result, for Marowitz, the play 'had stopped *meaning*'. Though we 'snicker at eighteenth-century "improvements" which distorted Shakespeare's plays', such, he argued, were defensible. Peter Brook, in chopping out the servants after Gloucester's blinding (see section 5 above, on 'Relevance') was doing something in the same tradition. All cutting, of course, affects meaning. Thus, when Hall cut some 75 of Horatio's lines, it was said by some critics that this had the effect of making Hamlet seem more isolated than Shakespeare had dramatised him. Marowitz went further, excising Horatio altogether, because he hung around 'like an insufferable feed' – a 'feed' being a music-hall comedian's stooge.

As part of his process of declassicisation, Marowitz developed the music-hall elements he found in the play. He built up Rosencrantz and Guildenstern into a sort of Morecambe and Wise act. When they 'dance on' for the first time they are described as a vaudeville team and are 'linked by a long rope'. There is a music-hall schoolroom act vaguely reminiscent of Will Hay with the Queen as teacher. Here they rework Polonius's advice to Laertes [I iii 58–61]:

Queen (as teacher) Come, come and sit you down
And these few precepts in thy memory

See thou character.
*Laertes, Ophelia and the Clown sit down in a line in front of Hamlet.
Teacher and class stand beating out the iambic rhythm with their fingers
against their palms, and the next is chanted out in a strictly scanned
sing-song.*
Give thy thoughts . . . *(Points to Ophelia).*
Ophelia No tongue.
Queen Nor any unproportioned thought is . . . *(to Hamlet).*
Hamlet Act.
Queen Be thou familiar but . . .
Clown (brightly, teacher's pet) By no means vulgar.

Marowitz builds on the audience's familiarity with the play.
What is said is thus intended to strike them afresh and to
suggest new implications and a new relevance. One or two
examples will make the technique plain. This is the effect of
combining III ii 383–6 and III i 120:

Hamlet Do you see that cloud that's almost in shape like a camel?
Polonius (studying it) By the mass, and it's like a camel indeed.
Hamlet Methinks it is like a weasel.
Ophelia I was the more deceived.

Hamlet, in his Advice to the Players, complained of Clowns
speaking more than was set down for them. Marowitz has the
Clown offer advice. The section begins with the Ghost, his arm
about Fortinbras, confiding in him, speaking colloquially:

If thou didst ever thy dear father love
Revenge his foul and most unnatural murder.
Fortinbras (imitating Hamlet) Haste, haste me to know it
That I with wings as swift . . .
Hamlet (seeing his place usurped by Fortinbras)
As meditation or the thoughts of love
May sweep to my revenge.
*Repeating speech, both play child's game – fist over fist – to win the toy
sword. Hamlet wins then leaps forward gallantly.*
Hamlet (centre stage; consciously performing)
Rightly to be great
Is not to stir without great argument.
Clown (with script, like exasperated director) Speak the speech, I pray
you, as I pronounced it to you, trippingly on the tongue.

> *Hamlet* But greatly to find quarrel in a straw . . .
> *Clown* Nor do not saw the air too much with your hand thus, but use
> all gently.
> *Hamlet* . . . greatly to find quarrel in a straw . . .

Shortly after, Ophelia and Gertrude are compounded in one:

> *King* Pretty Ophelia. *(The kiss – and the scene dissolves).*
> *Clown (as prompter)* A father killed . . . a mother stained . . . *Hamlet,*
> *still transfixed by the scene, does not stir. As the movie lights come on again,*
> *the Queen is discovered in King's arms; Ophelia has vanished.*

A final example unites Hamlet's wish to kill the King with his
killing of Polonius:

> *Hamlet* O vengeance!
> *Stabs the King, who is kneeling before him. Blackout as his sword enters.*
> *Lights up. The King still praying, unhurt. Repeated twice. On third stab,*
> *Polonius falls forward.*
> *Polonius* Oh, I am slain! *(Falls forward, dead).*
> *All, crying like banshees, dash out leaving Hamlet, the dead Polonius, and*
> *the Queen, grief-stricken at the corpse.*
> *Hamlet* Dead for a ducat, dead.
> *Cut sharply into new scene.*
> *Ophelia* You are merry, my Lord?

Marowitz's *Collage* has fascinating suggestions of earlier and
later productions. One section is presented like an old-time
silent film ('against flicker-wheel effect'), though with dialogue;
that seems to look back to Olivier's use of silent-film technique
(see section 7 above). The 'duel of Speeches' that accompanies
the fight with wooden toy swords is reminiscent of the verbal
duels in Jonson's masques and Randolph's *Amyntas* (1630).
Much use is made of film technique (hence such terms as 'cut'
and 'dissolve'), and Marowitz also adapts film's technique of
parallel action so that two scenes take place simultaneously on
different parts of the stage. Hamlet's swinging on a rope (giving
point to the Queen's line, 'This bodiless creation') looks forward to Brook's 'trapeze' production of *A Midsummer Night's
Dream*. The very music-hall Fool in the RSC *King Lear* (1982) – a
brilliantly conceived and executed characterisation – was also
anticipated in the *Collage*.

It would be wrong to lump Marowitz's *Collage* with the burlesques so fashionable in the nineteenth century. Marowitz's concern is at least as serious as was Murphy's in defending Shakespeare in his *Hamlet with Alterations*. What also marks it off from burlesque is its redeployment of Shakespeare's own language. What is Marowitz up to? How justified is he? Early in his Introduction to the Penguin edition he asks:

> Can a play which is very well known be reconstructed and redistributed so as to make a new work of art? If *Hamlet* were a precious old vase which shattered into a thousand pieces, could one glue the pieces all together into a completely new shape and still retain the spirit of the original?

A little later he suggests a criterion for what he has done: 'One of the questions behind the present undertaking is to discover to what extent one can juggle *those* elements and still maintain contact with what is essential in *Hamlet*.' He claims that 'Once the narrative sequence is broken, one has direct access to the play's ambiences. One rips open the golden lid of the treasure chest to find other riches within.' There is, perhaps, truth in this but inexcusably Marowitz goes on to justify what he has done by an analogy with rape:

> A spliced-up *Hamlet* doesn't destroy the play forever; just as a beautiful woman who is raped isn't barred from future domestic felicity. One might argue she is never the same woman afterwards, but is that necessarily a bad thing?

This astonishing judgement comes near to undermining – exposing – what Marowitz is up to. At bottom (see p. 40) he is concerned to indict what he sees as disreputable in our society, especially as validated by such a work as Shakespeare's *Hamlet*. Thus must Hamlet be pilloried, for Hamlet, says Marowitz, like many contemporary intellectuals, equates the taking of a position with the performance of an action. Marowitz's Hamlet is fashioned to earn our contempt, not to win our sympathy. Thus is the determination of Laertes directly contrasted with Hamlet's vacillation:

Laertes (suddenly) Where is my father?
King Dead.

Laertes I'll not be juggled with.
   To hell allegiance; vows to the blackest devil.
Hamlet (weakly trying to match Laertes's passion)
   Yes, from the table of my memory
   I'll wipe away all trivial fond records . . .
Laertes Conscience and grace to the profoundest pit.
Hamlet All saws of books, all forms, all pressures past.
Laertes I dare damnation.
Hamlet I have sworn it.

Marowitz undermines Hamlet and what troubles him even more seriously by showing him preferring to reflect rather than act at a moment when, as reconstructed by Marowitz, even the mildest might be expected to be provoked to action. The Queen is 'scooped up into the King's arms, and he proceeds to kiss and undress her'. The Ghost steps down from a picture-frame (in the manner of *Ruddigore*) and directs his 'O Hamlet, what a falling-off was there' [I v 47–52] to the embracing couple. He then addresses two lines to Hamlet [from I v 80–1]:

> O horrible, horrible, most horrible
> If thou hast nature in thee bear it not.

But Hamlet, 'trying not to see the King and Queen making love before his eyes', can only launch into 'I have of late . . . Why, it appears no other things to me than a foul and pestilent congregation of vapours' [II ii 297–303].
   Is this an 'indirect way of making contact with that work's essence' as Marowitz claims? Or is it a rape? Or can the *Collage* prompt in us a new understanding of Shakespeare's play and some insight into the condition of our society, whether or not we accept Marowitz's interpretation? Does Marowitz's attempt to indict the failings of society merely trivialise Shakespeare's dramatisation of the experience of mortality? Or do we return to Shakespeare, more aware, more capable of understanding, and refreshed?

READING LIST

The text of *Hamlet* quoted is the New Penguin Shakespeare edition (1980) edited by T. J. B. Spencer. The Introduction, by Anne Barton, influenced the 1980 RSC production. The most thorough edition is the New Arden, edited by Harold Jenkins (1982). This gives a very sane account of the relationship of the different versions and has splendid notes. Another useful edition is that prepared by Cyrus Hoy for Norton (New York, 1963). It has useful extracts from works by Shakespeare's contemporaries (on melancholy, demonology, nature of man, and ghosts) and from critical essays.

The Macmillan Casebook series has a very useful volume on *Hamlet*, ed. John Jump (1968) from which a number of passages have been quoted here. There are extracts from such as Voltaire, Johnson, Goethe, Hazlitt, G. H. Lewes, T. S. Eliot, Wilson Knight and Caroline Spurgeon, a dozen recent studies, and a bibliography; the essays by Ernest Jones, Maynard Mack, Harry Levin and Patrick Cruttwell will be found particularly helpful.

Shakespeare Survey, 9 (Cambridge UP, 1956) is devoted to *Hamlet* and includes an excellent survey of work on the play by Clifford Leech and an account of '*Hamlet* at the Comédie Française: 1769–1896' by Paul Benchettrit. More on French responses will be found in Marion Monaco, *Shakespeare and the French Stage in the Eighteenth Century* (Didier: Paris, 1974).

S. L. Bethell's *Shakespeare and the Popular Dramatic Tradition* (1944) has been reprinted in Vol. 8 of *Literary Taste, Culture and Mass Communications* ed. P. Davison, R. Meyersohn, and E. Shils (Chadwyck Healey: Cambridge, 1978). Richard David's *Shakespeare in the Theatre* (Cambridge UP, 1978) is an informative illustrated survey of major English productions of the 1970s. The splendid resources of The Shakespeare Centre, Stratford-upon-Avon, include RSC prompt-books and volumes of newspaper cuttings. It also holds Norman Cockin's detailed thesis, *Post-War Productions of 'Hamlet' at Stratford-upon-Avon, 1948–1974* (University of Birmingham, 1980).

J. M. Nosworthy's *Shakespeare's Occasional Plays* (Arnold, 1965) advances his theory about the origins of *Hamlet*. David Garrick's version has been edited, with an excellent commentary, by H. W. Pedicord and F. L. Bergmann in Vol. 4 of their edition of *The Plays of David Garrick* (Carbondale, Ill., 1981). My references are to that edition and commentary.

The Film Hamlet, ed. Brenda Cross (Saturn Press, 1948) is an illustrated record of the production with contributions by Olivier and those who made and acted in the film. Roger Manvell's broadcast was printed in *The Penguin Film Review*, 8 (1949). *Focus on Shakespearean Films*, ed. C. W. Eckert (Englewood Cliffs, NJ, 1972) has five essays on Olivier's and Kozintsev's film versions of *Hamlet*.

The two books drawn on for discussion of the Gielgud and Burton productions were Rosamond Gilder, *John Gielgud's Hamlet* (Methuen 1937), illustrated and with Gielgud's 'The Hamlet Tradition'. This is well worth tracking down for both these sections. Richard L. Sterne's *John Gielgud directs Richard Burton in 'Hamlet'* (Heinemann, 1968), is illustrated, includes extracts from newspaper criticisms in Toronto and New York, and has some set diagrams. The recording of the performance is Columbia DOL 302–4 and stereo DOS 702.

Stanley Wells's lecture on Peter Hall's *Hamlet* is printed in *Royal Shakespeare: Four Major Productions at Stratford-upon-Avon* (Manchester UP, 1977), pp. 23–42. Dr Wells provides background information on the production, gives fascinating details of stage business, and analyses the 'fall of a sparrow' dialogue in v ii both for its critical interpretation and its stage presentation.

Charles Marowitz's *Collage Hamlet* was published by Penguin in 1970 with his version of Marlowe's *Doctor Faustus*. It has an extremely useful introduction. In 1978 *The Marowitz Shakespeare* was published (Marion Boyars, London). This contains his *Hamlet Collage* and four more of Shakespeare's plays, also with an introduction. Marowitz's 'Lear Log' appeared in *Tulane Drama Review*, 22 (1963), and is still available in print. Another controversial *Hamlet* that might be followed up is that by Joseph Papp, his *'Naked' Hamlet* (see IV vii 50), published by Macmillan Inc. (New York, 1969). This is illustrated and has the music for the songs.

INDEX OF NAMES

Peter Davison

HAMLET: TEXT AND PERFORMANCE

This volume in the 'Text & Performance' series shows how *Hamlet* works
as drama and how the text is realised through performance.

Those who have studied and those who have performed this long and
puzzling play have moulded it quite remarkably to bring out the
experience it has to offer us, or to invest it with their conceptions of
Shakespeare and of life itself. Professor Davison examines the ways in
which - since Shakespeare's day and especially in our own times - the text
and the performance of *Hamlet* (and the Hamlet character) have been
inter-related. His survey, combining an appraisal of critical views on the
text with analyses of major theatrical productions, identifies themes and
problems of interpretation which are of concern to literary student,
theatre-goer and performer alike.

Peter Davison has held professorial appointments at St David's University
College and at the University of Kent at Canterbury. His many publications
include editions of plays by Shakespeare and his contemporaries, *Popular
Appeal in English Drama to 1859* and *Contemporary Drama and the
Popular Dramatic Tradition.*

The 'Text and Performance' series is designed to introduce students and
the general reader to the themes, continuing vitality and performance of
major dramatic texts. The attention given to production aspects is of
special importance, responding to the invigoration of literary study by the
work of leading contemporary critics and performers of drama. The prime
aim - achieved by analysis of the text in relation to its themes and
theatricality - is to present each play as a vital experience in the mind of
reader and spectator. Each volume has two parts. In Part One - *Text* -
certain basic problems or themes are discussed. Part Two - *Performance* -
examines the ways in which these problems or themes have been handled
in modern productions.

Michael Scott, General Editor of the series, is Principal Lecturer in English
Studies, Sunderland Polytechnic. His publications include *John Marston's
Plays: Theme, Structure and Performance* (1978); *Renaissance Drama and
a Modern Audience* (1982); and the volume on *Antony and Cleopatra* in
the series.

The cover illustration shows a rehearsal of Henry IV, Part 2. Photo: Zoë Dominic.

ISBN 0 333 33994 0